SENIOR CONSULTING EDITOR

SENATOR DANIEL PATRICK MOYNIHAN

CONSULTING EDITORS

ANN ORLOV
Managing Editor, *Harvard Encyclopedia of American Ethnic Groups*

M. MARK STOLARIK
President, The Balch Institute for Ethnic Studies, Philadelphia

DAVID M. REIMERS
Professor of History, New York University

JAMES F. WATTS
Chairman, History Department, City College of New York

The Peoples of North America

Kevin Osborn

CHELSEA HOUSE PUBLISHERS
New York Philadelphia

On the cover: A 1939 photograph of a Ukrainian school orchestra in Smokey Lake, Alberta, Canada.

CHELSEA HOUSE PUBLISHERS
Editor-in-Chief: Nancy Toff
Executive Editor: Remmel T. Nunn
Managing Editor: Karyn Gullen Browne
Copy Chief: Juliann Barbato
Picture Editor: Adrian G. Allen
Art Director: Maria Epes
Manufacturing Manager: Gerald Levine

The Peoples of North America
Senior Editor: Sean Dolan

Staff for THE UKRAINIAN AMERICANS
Associate Editor: Abigail Meisel
Deputy Copy Chief: Ellen Scordato
Editorial Assistant: Elizabeth Nix
Picture Research: PAR/NYC
Assistant Art Director: Laurie Jewell
Senior Designer: Noreen M. Lamb
Layout: Arlene Goldberg
Production Coordinator: Joseph Romano
Cover Illustration: Paul Biniasz
Banner Design: Hrana L. Janto

Copyright © 1989 by Chelsea House Publishers, a division of Main Line Book Co. All rights reserved. Printed and bound in the United States of America.

First Printing

1 3 5 7 9 8 6 4 2

Library of Congress Cataloging-in-Publication Data
Osborn, Kevin.
   The Ukrainian Americans / Kevin Osborn.
      p.   cm.—(The Peoples of North America)
   Bibliography: p.
   Includes index.
   Summary: Discusses the history, culture, and religion of the Ukrainians, factors encouraging their emigration, and their acceptance as an ethnic group in North America.
   ISBN 1-55546-138-7
       0-7910-0307-8 (pbk.)
   1. Ukrainian Americans—Juvenile literature.   [1. Ukrainian Americans.] I. Title. II. Series.   87-36976
E184.U5076 1988   CIP
973′.0491791—dc19   AC

Contents

Introduction: "A Nation of Nations"	7
Who Are the Ukrainians?	13
No Nation of Their Own	17
Leaving the Village Behind	37
No Streets Paved with Gold	47
Picture Essay: A Celebration of Tradition	49
A Society Within a Society	69
A Different Kind of Immigrant	85
Preservation Versus Assimilation	91
Progress and Tradition	99
Further Reading	108
Index	109

THE PEOPLES OF NORTH AMERICA

The Immigrant Experience
Illegal Aliens
Immigrants Who Returned Home
The Afro-Americans
The American Indians
The Amish
The Arab Americans
The Armenian Americans
The Baltic Americans
The Bulgarian Americans
The Carpatho-Rusyn Americans
The Central Americans
The Chinese Americans
The Croatian Americans
The Cuban Americans
The Czech Americans
The Danish Americans
The Dominican Americans
The Dutch Americans
The English Americans
The Filipino Americans
The French Americans
The French Canadians
The German Americans
The Greek Americans
The Haitian Americans
The Hungarian Americans
The Iberian Americans
The Indo-Americans
The Indo-Chinese Americans
The Iranian Americans
The Irish Americans
The Italian Americans
The Japanese Americans
The Jewish Americans
The Korean Americans
The Mexican Americans
The Norwegian Americans
The Pacific Islanders
The Peoples of the Arctic
The Polish Americans
The Puerto Ricans
The Romanian Americans
The Russian Americans
The Scotch-Irish Americans
The Scottish Americans
The Serbian Americans
The Slovak Americans
The South Americans
The Swedish Americans
The Turkish Americans
The Ukrainian Americans
The West Indian Americans

CHELSEA HOUSE PUBLISHERS

A NATION OF NATIONS

Daniel Patrick Moynihan

The Constitution of the United States begins: "We the People of the United States . . ." Yet, as we know, the United States is not made up of a single group of people. It is made up of many peoples. Immigrants from Europe, Asia, Africa, and Central and South America settled in North America seeking a new life filled with opportunities unavailable in their homeland. Coming from many nations, they forged one nation and made it their own. More than 100 years ago, Walt Whitman expressed this perception of America as a melting pot: "Here is not merely a nation, but a teeming Nation of nations."

Although the ingenuity and acts of courage of these immigrants, our ancestors, shaped the North American way of life, we sometimes take their contributions for granted. This fine series, *The Peoples of North America*, examines the experiences and contributions of the immigrants and how these contributions determined the future of the United States and Canada.

Immigrants did not abandon their ethnic traditions when they reached the shores of North America. Each ethnic group had its own customs and traditions, and each brought different experiences, accomplishments, skills, values, styles of dress, and tastes in food that lingered long after its arrival. Yet this profusion of differences created a singularity, or bond, among the immigrants.

The United States and Canada are unusual in this respect. Whereas religious and ethnic differences have sparked intolerance throughout the rest of the world—from the 17th-century religious wars to the 19th-century nationalist movements in Europe to the near extermination of the Jewish people under Nazi Germany—North Americans have struggled to learn how to respect each other's differences and live in harmony.

Millions of immigrants from scores of homelands brought diversity to our continent. In a mass migration, some 12 million immigrants passed through the waiting rooms of New York's Ellis Island; thousands more came to the West Coast. At first, these immigrants were welcomed because labor was needed to meet the demands of the Industrial Age. Soon, however, the new immigrants faced the prejudice of earlier immigrants who saw them as a burden on the economy. Legislation was passed to limit immigration. The Chinese Exclusion Act of 1882 was among the first laws closing the doors to the promise of America. The Japanese were also effectively excluded by this law. In 1924, Congress set immigration quotas on a country-by-country basis.

Such prejudices might have triggered war, as they did in Europe, but North Americans chose negotiation and compromise, instead. This determination to resolve differences peacefully has been the hallmark of the peoples of North America.

The remarkable ability of Americans to live together as one people was seriously threatened by the issue of slavery. It was a symptom of growing intolerance in the world. Thousands of settlers from the British Isles had arrived in the colonies as indentured servants, agreeing to work for a specified number of years on farms or as apprentices in return for passage to America and room and board. When the first Africans arrived in the then-British colonies during the 17th century, some colonists thought that they too should be treated as indentured servants. Eventually, the question of whether the Africans should be viewed as indentured, like the English, or as slaves who could be owned for life, was considered in a Maryland court. The court's calamitous decree held that blacks were slaves bound to lifelong servitude, and so were their children.

America went through a time of moral examination and civil war before it finally freed African slaves and their descendants. The principle that all people are created equal had faced its greatest challenge and survived.

Yet the court ruling that set blacks apart from other races fanned flames of discrimination that burned long after slavery was abolished—and that still flicker today. The concept of racism had existed for centuries in countries throughout the world. For instance, when the Manchus conquered China in the 17th century, they decreed that Chinese and Manchus could not intermarry. To impress their superiority on the conquered Chinese, the Manchus ordered all Chinese men to wear their hair in a long braid called a queue.

By the 19th century, some intellectuals took up the banner of racism, citing Charles Darwin. Darwin's scientific studies hypothesized that highly evolved animals were dominant over other animals. Some advocates of this theory applied it to humans, asserting that certain races were more highly evolved than others and thus were superior.

This philosophy served as the basis for a new form of discrimination, not only against nonwhite people but also against various ethnic groups. Asians faced harsh discrimination and were depicted by popular 19th-century newspaper cartoonists as depraved, degenerate, and deficient in intelligence. When the Irish flooded American cities to escape the famine in Ireland, the cartoonists caricatured the typical "Paddy" (a common term for Irish immigrants) as an apelike creature with jutting jaw and sloping forehead.

By the 20th century, racism and ethnic prejudice had given rise to virulent theories of a Northern European master race. When Adolf Hitler came to power in Germany in 1933, he popularized the notion of Aryan supremacy. "Aryan," a term referring to the Indo-European races, was applied to so-called superior physical characteristics such as blond hair, blue eyes, and delicate facial features. Anyone with darker and heavier features was considered inferior. Buttressed by these theories, the German Nazi state from

1933 to 1945 set out to destroy European Jews, along with Poles, Russians, and other groups considered inferior. It nearly succeeded. Millions of these people were exterminated.

The tragedies brought on by ethnic and racial intolerance throughout the world demonstrate the importance of North America's efforts to create a society free of prejudice and inequality.

A relatively recent example of the New World's desire to resolve ethnic friction nonviolently is the solution the Canadians found to a conflict between two ethnic groups. A long-standing dispute as to whether Canadian culture was properly English or French resurfaced in the mid-1960s, dividing the peoples of the French-speaking Quebec Province from those of the English-speaking provinces. Relations grew tense, then bitter, then violent. The Royal Commission on Bilingualism and Biculturalism was established to study the growing crisis and to propose measures to ease the tensions. As a result of the commission's recommendations, all official documents and statements from the national government's capital at Ottawa are now issued in both French and English, and bilingual education is encouraged.

The year 1980 marked a coming of age for the United States's ethnic heritage. For the first time, the U.S. Census asked people about their ethnic background. Americans chose from more than 100 groups, including French Basque, Spanish Basque, French Canadian, Afro-American, Peruvian, Armenian, Chinese, and Japanese. The ethnic group with the largest response was English (49.6 million). More than 100 million Americans claimed ancestors from the British Isles, which includes England, Ireland, Wales, and Scotland. There were almost as many Germans (49.2 million) as English. The Irish-American population (40.2 million) was third, but the next largest ethnic group, the Afro-Americans, was a distant fourth (21 million). There was a sizable group of French ancestry (13 million), as well as of Italian (12 million). Poles, Dutch, Swedes, Norwegians, and Russians followed. These groups, and other smaller ones, represent the wondrous profusion of ethnic influences in North America.

Canada, too, has learned more about the diversity of its population. Studies conducted during the French/English conflict showed that Canadians were descended from Ukrainians, Germans, Italians, Chinese, Japanese, native Indians, and Eskimos, among others. Canada found it had no ethnic majority, although nearly half of its immigrant population had come from the British Isles. Canada, like the United States, is a land of immigrants for whom mutual tolerance is a matter of reason as well as principle.

The people of North America are the descendants of one of the greatest migrations in history. And that migration is not over. Koreans, Vietnamese, Nicaraguans, Cubans, and many others are heading for the shores of North America in large numbers. This mix of cultures shapes every aspect of our lives. To understand ourselves, we must know something about our diverse ethnic ancestry. Nothing so defines the North American nations as the motto on the Great Seal of the United States: *E Pluribus Unum*—Out of Many, One.

A Ukrainian-American family in the Canadian province of Alberta enjoys a temporary respite from its labors in September 1941. The majority of Ukrainian immigrants in Canada settled on farms.

WHO ARE THE UKRAINIANS?

Although patriotic Ukrainians have long thought of their homeland as an independent nation, the Ukraine has enjoyed only four years of independence since the 18th century. During that period its various regions have fallen under the sway of Poland, Austria-Hungary, Czechoslovakia, and Russia and the Soviet Union. Thus, although they spoke their own language, had distinct religious beliefs and practices and a rich culture, many Ukrainians who came to North America to settle were labeled—and often thought of themselves—as Russian, Austrian, Hungarian, Polish, or Czech.

The 1980 U.S. census reported that 730,056 Americans claimed partial Ukrainian descent, and 381,084 of these reported it as their only ancestry. Many others, unaware of their true lineage, listed other nationalities instead. Should these people be included in an estimate of the Ukrainian-American population? At this point in history, the answer must be no. Ukrainians, once identified by geographical origin, can now identify themselves only through their language, their religions—primarily Ukrainian Catholicism and Ukrainian Orthodoxy—and their culture and traditions.

Today, most Ukrainian Americans still live near the same places where their ancestors first settled. More than 55 percent of all Ukrainian Americans live in the northeastern United States. Forty-eight percent live in Pennsylvania, New York, or New Jersey. (Pennsylvania and New Jersey are the only states in which more than one percent of the population call themselves Ukrainian Americans.) Other states with large Ukrainian-American populations include California, Michigan, Ohio, Illinois, Connecticut, and Florida. The other 41 states combined have fewer Ukrainian Americans than Pennsylvania alone.

Many Ukrainian Americans still reside in the urban centers—or the outlying suburbs—where early Ukrainian immigrants lived so as to be near the factories and industries where they worked. Pittsburgh, Philadelphia, New York City, Baltimore, Detroit—and in Canada, Toronto and Winnipeg—head the roster of cities that still have thriving and highly visible Ukrainian communities. Other members of the group, especially in central and western Canada, still live in the rural areas where their ancestors established farms and homes.

In the late 1800s and the early years of the 20th century, Ukrainian Americans helped extend the settled regions of the United States and Canada to the West Coast. Ukrainian Americans were among the first pioneers to arrive in the northwestern United States, and in their search for farmland, Ukrainian immigrants helped push Canada's borders to the Pacific Ocean. Ukrainian Americans also played an instrumental role in the growth of the labor movement, helping to form unions that have improved working conditions in both the United States and Canada. In fact, there are few fields in which members of this immigrant group have not distinguished themselves. Science, business, academics, the arts, sports, and entertainment have all profited from the contributions of Ukrainian Americans. Indeed, the typical Ukrainian American of today is so

successful that the median income of members of this immigrant group is 12 percent higher than the national average. This achievement becomes even more remarkable when one considers that the majority of Ukrainians who came to America were illiterate—not only in English, but in Ukrainian as well. Prosperity came after a long and difficult struggle.

Although most had been farmers in the old country, a great number of Ukrainians found work as coal miners in the New World.

The Ukraine's rich grain harvests resulted in its being known as the "breadbasket of Europe." These two women are reading a newspaper during their work break.

No Nation of Their Own

The history of the Ukrainian people has been—and remains—a ceaseless battle for independence. Since the 13th century, when hordes of Mongols first invaded the land, the Ukraine has enjoyed only brief periods of self-rule. Its oppressors have included bordering countries—Poland, Russia, Hungary, Czechoslovakia, and Romania—and more distant ones, such as Germany and Austria. Although today the region has its own seat at the United Nations—a privilege granted, in theory, only to independent states—it enjoys no more autonomy than any of the other 14 republics that together with the Ukraine make up the Union of Soviet Socialist Republics (USSR).

Located along the Black Sea in the southwestern region of the USSR, the Ukraine is both immense and populous. Its 233,000 square miles exceed the total area of France by 10 percent, and among the nations of Europe only the Soviet Union surpasses it in size. Its fertile soil, ideal for growing grain, supports a population that in the 1980s exceeded 50 million, a number bettered by only 5 European countries. (In addition to ethnic Ukrainians, this figure includes some 13 million Russians and other nonethnic Ukrainians.)

The Ukraine has traditionally been called the "breadbasket of Europe" and also boasts an abundance of natural resources, including large deposits of coal,

UKRAINE AND SURROUNDING AREA

iron, and other metals. Thirteen percent of the world's iron reserves are located in the Ukraine, and the region produces almost 35 percent of the Soviet Union's coal.

The Ukrainian people are descendants of various tribes that probably migrated from the basin of the Vistula, Dniester, and Pripet rivers, in what is now southeastern Poland, and settled in the region in the 1st century A.D. Gradually these tribes developed into a "family" of Slavic peoples, including the Ukrainians, Russians, Poles, Czechs, Slovaks, Serbs, Bulgarians, Croatians, and others. Today, Ukrainians form the second largest Slavic group, surpassed in number only by their ethnic cousins, the Russians. Like them, the Ukrainians use the Cyrillic rather than the Arabic alphabet used throughout the Western hemisphere, but the Ukrainians have a unique language and a culture distinct from other Slavic groups. They have fought to preserve this cultural distinctness for centuries.

Kievan Russia: The First Independent Ukrainian State

The Greek historian Herodotus, who lived in the 5th century B.C., is responsible for what is the oldest existing written reference to what is now known as the Ukraine. Called "the Father of History," Herodotus referred to the land as Scythia, after the tribe that lived there and traded with the Greeks. Later, other nomadic tribes briefly occupied the territory. In the 3rd century A.D, the Goths, a Germanic tribe that later overran the Roman Empire, inhabited the Ukraine before being driven out by the Huns. Once the Huns moved on, continuing westward on their path of conquest, Slavic tribes began to establish themselves on the region's grassy steppes. They founded the city of Kiev, on the

The Scythians, the pre-Slavic inhabitants of the Ukraine, crafted this 4th-century B.C. silver cup, found in an archaeological excavation near Nikopol.

A stunning example of classic Byzantine architecture, St. Sophia's Cathedral in Kiev was built in 1037.

Dnieper River, which by the 5th century was an important outpost on the river trade routes between Constantinople and the Baltic Sea.

The modern Russian state, as generally agreed, dates to about 862, when Rurik, a Viking prince, established his capital at Novgorod. This event was to have profound implications for the history of the Ukraine. Expanding along the Dnieper and other trade routes, the Viking kingdom soon came into contact with the Slavic tribes to the south. Oleg, a successor to Rurik, seized Kiev in 882; but instead of imposing their own customs on the Ukraine, the new conquerors seem to have embraced the language and traditions of the native peoples, the Rus.

Kievan Russia became the first significant Slavic empire. Under Vladimir I, who ruled from approximately 980 to 1015, Kievan Russia won military victories over Lithuania, Bulgaria, and the Greek-controlled Crimean peninsula on the Black Sea. These triumphs enlarged the empire until it encompassed more than 1.2 million square miles between the Black and Baltic seas.

It was Vladimir who established Christianity as the religion of the Ukraine. Like many other inhabitants of Kievan Russia, Vladimir was converted to Christianity by missionaries from Greece. More tolerant than many of the church's emissaries, these Greek missionaries allowed their converts to use the Old Slavonic language in worship and ceremonies and to mingle traditional Ukrainian religious customs and practices, such as a married priesthood, with the rites of the new faith. The missionaries also introduced the Byzantine style of architecture to Kievan Russia. (Byzantium, the ancient name for Constantinople, was then the capital of the Eastern Roman Empire and one of the seats of the Greek Orthodox church.) A church built in the Byzantine style typically featured a central domed space as well as several other areas topped by a dome or half-dome. Byzantine architecture would characterize Ukrainian churches for centuries to come.

Yaroslav the Wise succeeded Vladimir in 1019. He supervised the development of the Slavic world's first written code of laws, the *Russkaya Pravda*, or Russian Truth, and supported the spread of Christianity. Under Yaroslav, Kievan Russia became a complex political entity. Its government combined elements of monarchy, aristocracy, and democracy. Control of the state was divided among the prince (Yaroslav himself), a select group of royal landowners known as *boyars*, and an assembly of representatives elected by free citizens—those who did not serve the nobility as serfs (agricultural laborers legally bound to their master's land.)

Kievan Russia reached its cultural and economic zenith under Yaroslav, but in the two centuries following his death, its power waned. Royal heirs battled for ascendancy, splintering the ruling house of Rurik and breaking the empire into smaller and smaller regions, each ruled by a different branch of the royal family. Internal conflict was not limited to political matters. The rift between the eastern and western branches of Catholicism evolved into a permanent split. The chief difference between the two sects, which remained closely similar in doctrine, concerned their interpretation of the spiritual and ecumenical authority of the pope. The western branch, or the Roman Catholics, believed the pope to be supreme head of the church and regarded him as personally infallible when speaking or ruling on church doctrine. Eastern Orthodox Catholics regarded the pope as the bishop of Rome, one of the five patriarchates into which the church was divided. (The others were Constantinople, Alexandria, Antioch, and Jerusalem.) Although the pope enjoyed some distinction among Eastern Orthodox adherents because he was considered the successor to Saint Peter, he was not believed to possess supreme authority. For Orthodox Catholics, infallibility resides in the church as a whole,

Yaroslav the Wise ruled over Kievan Russia at its political, cultural, and economic height.

as represented by the council of bishops, and not in the pope alone. After the split, the patriarch of Constantinople became the head of the Eastern church, and most worshipers in Kievan Russia continued to follow Orthodox rites.

Kievan Russia also faced external pressures. Much of the Ukraine came under the influence of the princes who ruled the western regions of Galicia and Volhynia, in what is now Poland. In 1240 Kiev was destroyed by the Mongols, led by Batu Khan, grandson of the celebrated warrior Genghis Khan, whose conquests stretched from Mongolia across the length of Asia to as far west as present-day Hungary. Batu Khan founded the empire known as the Golden Horde, which ruled much of southern and eastern Russia for the next 200 years.

The destruction of its capital city completed the disintegration of Kievan Russia. During this time, the cultural and linguistic differences between the disparate Slavic peoples had been deepening, giving rise to distinct ethnic groups and nations: the Ukrainians, the Russians, the Poles, and others. By the middle of the

Batu Khan's Mongol horsemen (right) clash with Hungarian cavalry at the Danube River in 1241. Batu founded the Empire of the Golden Horde, which ruled over what is now the Ukraine for nearly 200 years.

14th century, Poland had conquered Galicia, and Lithuania had annexed Volhynia. The eastern Ukraine remained under Mongol control.

Reign of the Cossacks

With the fall of Kievan Russia, Muscovy, or Moscow, became the most important Russian state. In 1480, Grand Prince Ivan III (called Ivan the Great) drove the Mongols from Muscovy and neighboring areas, including the Ukraine. Because most of the Ukrainian population had migrated to the west with the arrival of the Golden Horde, the Mongols' departure left the steppes in the east almost uninhabited. By the early days of the 16th century, however, Ukrainians had begun to return to the eastern regions, where they survived by trapping and hunting.

The eastern settlements were frequently raided by the fierce Tatars—Turkic descendants of the Mongols—who lived to the south, on the Crimean peninsula. To protect themselves, the settlers erected *sichs* (forts). Poland and Russia each desired to make the Ukraine their protectorate; both sent soldiers to man the frontier outposts against the Tatars and other invaders, and the sichs soon became the centers of organized military colonies. The soldiers, who received special privileges, came from a variety of ethnic backgrounds. Many were in trouble with the law, willing to give military service in exchange for relief from a jail sentence or debt. A great many were Ukrainian peasants from the west who had fled their Polish landlords. The inhabitants of these virtually autonomous military communities came to be known as Cossacks, from a Turkish word meaning outlaw.

Cossack communities were governed by a severe discipline, strictly enforced. Each member received a new name and instructions to forget all past designations of status or class. A Cossack sich organized its own *rada* (general assembly), which selected an *ataman* (commander) and a *hetman* (commander in chief). During

Petro Konashevych-Sahaydachny was a 17th-century Cossack commander, or hetman. The freedom-loving Cossacks helped expand the reaches of the Russian Empire.

times of war, Cossacks obeyed their ataman and hetman without question. Aside from these two, all the men in the sich (no women were allowed) were regarded as equals.

In the mid-16th century, the Cossacks formed their own free state in the southern Ukraine. Nominally under Polish rule, the inhabitants of Zaporizhska Sich, as the Cossack state was known, in fact enjoyed considerable freedom. They governed themselves and established their own institutions, even building new churches and schools. This autonomy contrasted sharply with the repression suffered by Ukrainians in the western provinces.

To combat the growing strength of Russia, Lithuania and Poland united under a single monarch in 1569. The two nations had traditionally taken different approaches toward their Ukrainian communities. Lithuania had formerly tolerated Ukrainian traditions and institutions, but Poland sought to destroy non-Polish ethnic cultures as a means of reinforcing the unity of its territories. The Ukrainian church came under special attack by the Roman Catholic Polish monarchs, who levied crippling taxes on individual churches and shut them down once their coffers were empty. The Ukrainian Orthodox church tried to appease Poland's royalty by joining with the Roman Catholic church in 1596, but it was a merger in name only. The new Ukrainian Catholic church retained many of the liturgies and customs of old—in particular, the right of priests to marry. Although the move won the support of the pope, who extended a welcome to members of the new Ukrainian church, it failed to satisfy the Polish nobility, who continued their campaign against Ukrainian religious practice. Recognizing that the merger had failed, many "converted" bishops broke away from the united Ukrainian church and returned to the Orthodox church.

During the first half of the 17th century, the Cossacks carried out several revolts against Poland, aided by the inhabitants of the western Ukraine and other

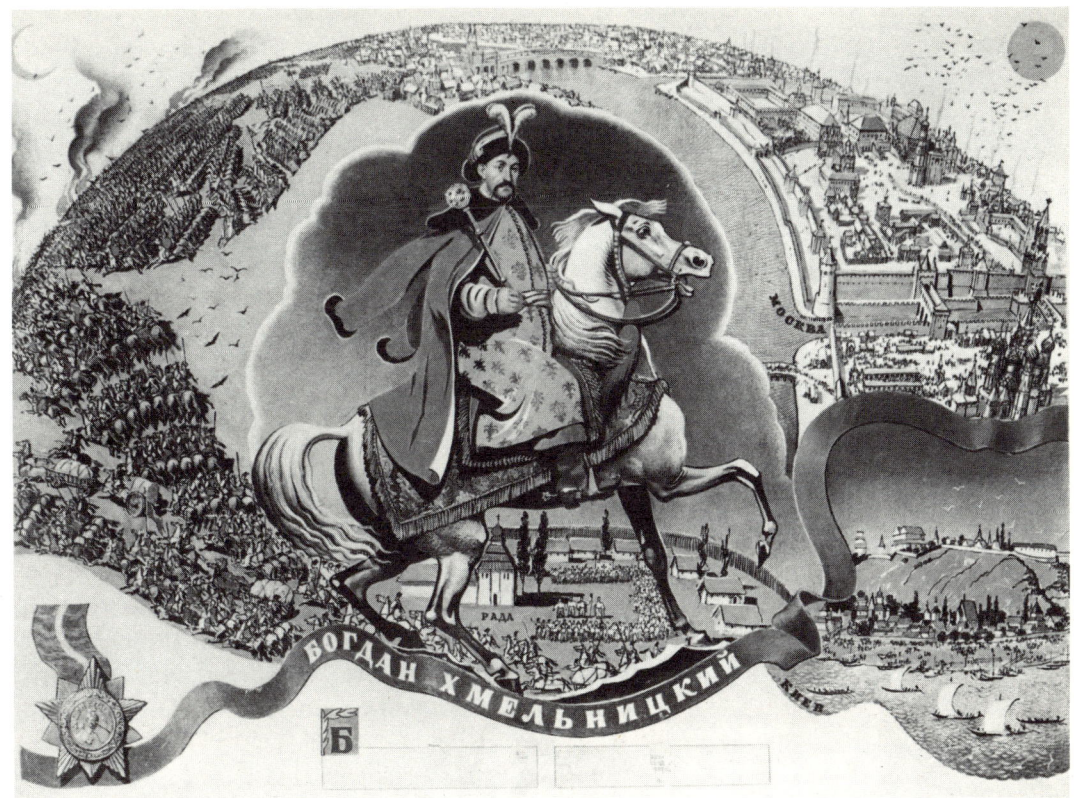

The Cossack hetman Bohdan Khmelnytsky liberated Ukrainian territory controlled by Poland and founded an independent Ukrainian nation.

groups dissatisfied with Polish rule. In 1649, Cossack forces under Hetman Bohdan Khmelnytsky defeated the Polish armies, reclaimed all Ukrainian territory under Polish rule, and established a separate and united Ukrainian nation. Threatened by both Poland and the Tatars, Khmelnytsky signed a treaty of protection with Czar Alexis I of Muscovy in 1654. The agreement stipulated political autonomy for the Ukraine, but the Russians almost immediately moved troops into the area, supposedly as a defense against Polish encroachment.

Bent on obtaining the region's independence, Khmelnytsky's successor, Hetman Ivan Vyhovsky, revoked the treaty in 1659 and marshaled forces that subdued the Russian troops. Having both been subdued by the Cossacks, Poland and Russia then united against the Ukraine, ushering in a period the Ukrainians call the epoch of ruins. After their combined forces routed the Cossacks in 1667, the two victors divided the

Czarina Catherine the Great, who ruled from 1762 to 1796, pursued imperialist policies that strengthened Russia's hold on the Ukraine.

Ukraine along the Dnieper River, with the Poles seizing the area to the west and the Russians claiming the eastern Ukraine. The Russians were as intent on eradicating Ukrainian culture and traditions as the Poles had been, and the Russian Orthodox church officially absorbed the Ukrainian Orthodox church in 1686.

It was not long before the Cossacks launched another attempt to establish an independent Ukrainian nation. A leader of the eastern Ukrainians, Hetman Ivan Mazepa, entered into a pact with King Charles XII of Sweden, who was competing with the Russians for territory along the Baltic Sea. The defeat of Charles's forces by the troops of Czar Peter I (called Peter the Great) in 1709 ended Mazepa's bid for Ukrainian sovereignty. Pockets of Cossack resistance remained, but in 1775, Catherine II (called Catherine the Great) crushed the last remaining Cossack stronghold, and in 1781, Russia formally annexed the eastern Ukraine. When Russia established colonies on Kodiak Island, which is now part of Alaska, in 1784, many of the settlers were Cossacks who had been imprisoned in Siberia for their resistance to Russian domination.

A People Under Domination

Unable to withstand the aggressive designs of its stronger neighbors, Poland was partitioned among Russia, Austria, and Prussia in 1795. All of its claims on the Ukraine were ceded to Russia, except for the three western provinces—Galicia, Bukovina, and the Carpatho-Ukraine—which came under Austrian control. Under Russian rule the Ukrainians continued to suffer political and cultural repression, with the church again the main target. In 1839, the Russian Orthodox church, supported by Czar Nicholas I, forced Ukrainians to worship in its own chapels rather than in those of the Ukrainian Orthodox church. Although Nicholas's successor, Alexander II, was a more enlightened ruler who in 1861 freed the serfs (agricultural servants legally bound to their master's land), the lot of his Ukrainian subjects did not improve appreciably. Alexander forbade publication of all Ukrainian-language books, newspapers, and journals. In the next decade, Alexander and the Russian Orthodox church began a program of coerced conversion aimed at members of various Protestant sects in the lands under Russian control, singling out the Stundinsts, a Ukrainian Baptist sect, for particular attention.

Despite the repression, the 19th century witnessed a Ukrainian cultural revival. The study of Ukrainian culture and folklore enjoyed a renewed popularity, and Ukrainian artists and intellectuals encouraged the creation of literature written in the vernacular. The Cyril and Methodius Society, founded by the Ukrainian poet Taras Shevchenko and named after the Greek missionaries who brought the Christian gospel to the Slavs, advocated Ukrainian nationalism. After the 1860s, its message was spread by secret *hromadas*, or communities. It was the growth of these hromadas that inspired Alexander II to proscribe Ukrainian-language publications. Ukrainians living in Austria, where the government was somewhat less autocratic, came to regard themselves as the protectors of Ukrainian culture and heritage. They organized societies that sponsored libraries, reading rooms, and choral or drama groups, as well as clubs and political organizations dedicated to the cause of Ukrainian independence.

A Taste of Freedom

Angered by military defeats, food shortages, and decades of autocratic government, the Russian people forced Czar Nicholas II to abdicate in March 1917. While a provisional government in the Russian capital, Petrograd (formerly Saint Petersburg), tried to establish order, a congress of representatives from all the provinces of the Ukraine elected their own parliament, known as the Rada. After the Bolsheviks (Communists) seized power from the provisional government in November 1917, their leader, Vladimir Ilyich Lenin, ordered the Rada to submit to the authority of the new government.

Czar Alexander II freed his nation's serfs but increased repression in the Ukraine. He was slain by an assassin's bomb in 1881.

The Rada refused to give in. Instead, it announced the formation of the Ukrainian National Republic and adopted a constitution that created a special cabinet post for each of the Ukraine's major ethnic groups, including the Poles and the Jews. The constitution also granted freedom to all political prisoners of the czar, abolished capital punishment, and redistributed the nation's land, most of which was owned by the nobility, by creating 81-acre plots to be farmed by peasants and their families. Although Russian nobles living in the Ukraine condemned the Rada's land redistribution program as "Bolshevik"—Lenin advocated an end to private ownership of property—the Bolsheviks liked it no better. They denounced it as "bourgeois" because the land would still be individually rather than collectively owned. Undaunted, the Rada went ahead with its plan, and on January 22, 1918, proclaimed the Ukrainian National Republic a free, independent, and sovereign state.

The new republic acted quickly to fortify itself by signing a treaty with Germany, Russia's enemy in World War I. The pact called for Germany to provide the Ukraine with military assistance against the Bolsheviks in exchange for shipments of grain, which Germany, its own food stores depleted by the war, badly needed. The expected Russian offensive was not long in coming. The Bolsheviks established their own government in the Ukrainian city of Kharkov and then marched into Kiev, but when Lenin signed the Treaty of Brest-Litovsk with Germany in March 1918, Russia withdrew from World War I and relinquished its claims on the Ukraine. With the immediate danger of Russian intervention gone, the Germans overthrew the Ukrainian Republic in April and installed their own puppet, General Paul Skoropadsky, as hetman. Almost immediately, the Germans reinstated the dispossessed Russian nobles to their estates.

Elsewhere, however, the war did not go well for Germany and its ally, Austria-Hungary. With the Aus-

On November 20, 1917, in Kiev, Ukrainians gather in the square before the church of St. Sophia to proclaim the Ukrainian National Republic.

tro-Hungarian Empire in ruins, the western Ukraine announced its independence and its intention to reunite with the Ukrainian National Republic on November 1, 1918. Ten days later World War I officially ended, and the defeated German troops, accompanied by many of the Russian nobles whom they had restored to power, began to withdraw from the Ukraine. The region was governed once again by the Rada, which reestablished the Ukrainian National Republic on December 24. On January 22, 1919, the Ukrainian National Republic and the Republic of the Western Ukraine united, bringing 35 million people under democratic rule. The new Ukrainian nation was led by Simon Petlyura.

The following month the Rada declared Ukrainian the official language of the new republic, but the people soon faced yet another threat to their independence. Russia was embroiled in a civil war between the Bolsheviks and their opponents, and both sides wished to claim the Ukraine. At the same time Poland, which had regained its independence at the end of World War I, launched a military campaign to recapture Galicia and Volhynia, its former colonies in the western Ukraine. The entire Ukraine became a battleground for warring forces. Poland added further to the confusion by extending diplomatic recognition to the Ukrainian National Republic. Less than a year later, Poland reversed itself and agreed with the Soviet Union, as Russia had

Bolshevik troops on parade in the Ukrainian city of Kharkov. Much of the fighting during the Russian civil war took place in the Ukraine.

been renamed, to partition the Ukraine. The Bolsheviks established a Soviet Ukrainian state, and Poland retained control over the western provinces. Other treaties signed as part of the World War I peace negotiations gave the Ukrainian regions of Bukovina to Romania and the Carpatho-Ukraine to Czechoslovakia. The short life of the Ukrainian National Republic had ended, a point the Soviets reinforced by executing 359 Ukrainian soldiers on November 21, 1921.

Years of Famine: The Ukrainian Soviet Socialist Republic

After the partition, the Ukraine was ruled by four separate foreign masters. Each imposed measures limiting, to various degrees, the political, intellectual, cultural, economic, and religious freedoms of Ukrainians. Perhaps most common were strictures on Ukrainian religious practices. The Poles sought to bring their subjects into the Roman Catholic church. Because the Soviet Union was now an atheist state—Karl Marx, the most important communist thinker and writer, had termed religion "the opium of the people"—any worship at all was strictly discouraged, and Ukrainian churches came under strict state regulation. The Romanians were more tolerant. They permitted the Ukrainians to worship as they pleased and to use their own language in church liturgy, although services had to be conducted in Romanian whenever a Romanian official attended.

Most of the Ukraine was controlled by the Soviet Union, and it was there that the Ukrainians endured the greatest repression. Although the Soviet constitution promised the cultural and political freedom of its constituent republics, few of its more than 100 ethnic minorities found such guarantees comforting, particularly once Lenin's successor, Joseph Stalin, instituted his policy of Russification, a program designed to ensure the ascendancy of the ethnic Russian majority and establish the control of the Communist party over virtually every aspect of life. Even those leaders in the Ukraine who belonged to the Communist party were stripped of power and replaced with non-Ukrainians.

A sign over the door of a Ukrainian church predicts the death of religion in five years. The Soviet Union imposed severe restrictions on Ukrainian religious practices.

Attempting to remake the economy, the Soviet government subjected virtually every aspect of industrial and agricultural production to state planning and regimentation. The planned economy proved particularly disastrous for the Ukraine, where a quota system on agricultural produce was introduced in 1921. The quota required that the peasant farmers of the Ukraine and other Soviet republics turn over to the government—at a specified price—a fixed quantity of crops from their annual harvests. The government price was not designed to earn the peasants a profit, and with the government controlling food distribution, there was little opportunity to sell their crops elsewhere. Their incentive reduced, Ukrainian farmers produced less, and the government took a large percentage of what they did grow. In 1921 and 1922, the "breadbasket of Europe" suffered a famine so severe that the Soviet government was forced to call upon other nations for relief.

In 1928, Stalin introduced his Five-Year Plan, a blueprint for the modernization and industrialization of the Soviet economy. A crucial element of Stalin's economic program was the collectivization of agriculture.

Corpses were stacked like cordwood at this Ukrainian cemetery during the famine of the 1930s. Some historians believe Soviet leader Joseph Stalin intentionally caused the famine to end resistance to collectivization.

This tractor station near Odessa controlled the distribution of modern agricultural machinery for use on the collective farms established by Stalin.

Private ownership of farmland was abolished; peasants in the Ukraine and elsewhere were driven from their individual plots to work as farmhands on huge, mechanized agricultural cooperatives. Resistance in the Ukraine was fierce. Many Ukrainian farmers slaughtered their own livestock rather than turn it over to the collective farms. Between 1928 and 1934, the Soviet horse population fell from 32 million to less than 16 million. In the first two months of 1930 alone, 14 million head of cattle were reportedly destroyed.

In March of that year, Stalin announced that compulsory collectivization had been a mistake and urged voluntary participation. Within two months the number of collectivized households in the country fell from 57.6 percent to 23.6 percent, and the government resumed its former policy of mandatory collectivization, using the army and police to force compliance. The state impounded land, cattle, farm implements, and homes. Opponents of collectivization were shot or deported to labor camps. Enforced by army seizures, the state quotas for Ukrainian crops rose from 26 percent to more than 50 percent in 1932. Severe famine was the result, beginning in 1932 and continuing in varying degrees for the rest of the decade. Between 4 and 7 million Ukrainians starved to death. During the 1930s Stalin's government also executed or imprisoned most of the Ukraine's political and cultural leaders.

When World War II began and the forces of Nazi Germany invaded the Ukraine, its inhabitants welcomed them as deliverers. Under the leadership of Stefan Bandera, the Organization of Ukrainian Nationalists proclaimed the rebirth of an independent Ukraine, but the Ukrainians soon learned that Nazis had come to conquer, not to liberate. The Germans executed Ukrainian nationalist leaders, deported Ukrainian workers to Austria and Germany for forced labor, and killed an estimated 850,000 Ukrainian Jews. In 1944, combined Soviet and U.S. forces drove the Germans from the Ukraine, and the region returned to Soviet control. At war's end the Ukraine was reunified when the Soviet Union annexed Bukovina from Romania, Galicia from Poland, and the Carpatho-Ukraine from Czechoslovakia.

While repression continued—strict restrictions on emigration were instituted, for example—Ukrainians

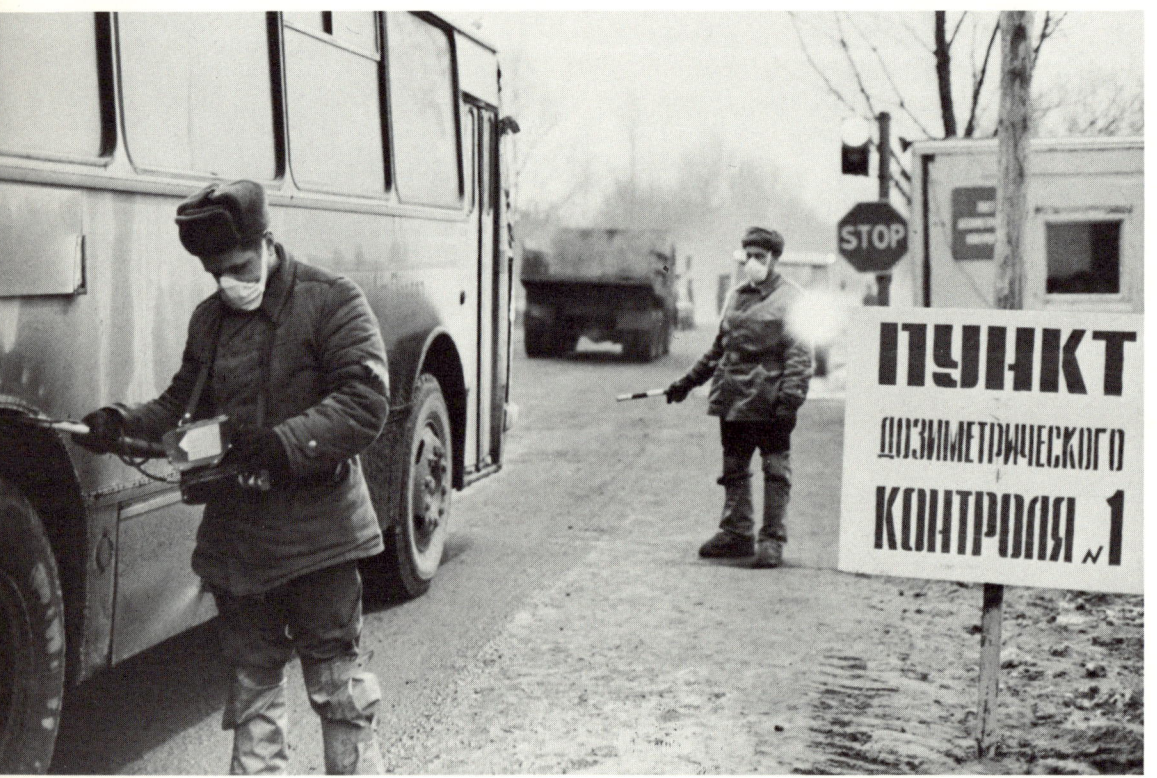

More than 19 months after the meltdown at the Chernobyl nuclear power plant in April 1986, masked technicians in the Ukraine were still testing vehicles for evidence of radiation.

came to play a more active role in regional and national government in the decades after the war, particularly following Stalin's death in 1953; Nikita Khrushchev, who succeeded Stalin as premier, was of Ukrainian peasant stock.

The Ukraine was also the site of the worst accident in the history of nuclear energy. On April 28, 1986, a meltdown occurred at the Chernobyl nuclear plant, 60 miles north of Kiev. The accident killed at least two, forced the uprooting of countless others, and released a cloud of radioactive contamination that spread over the other nations of Europe. It will take decades to assess the total damage that resulted.

Under Mikhail Gorbachev, who became the general secretary of the Communist party and the head of the Soviet Union in March 1985, Ukrainians have enjoyed more freedom of cultural expression and greater participation in their nation's government than at any time in their recent past, and the *perestroika* (restructuring) that Gorbachev has promised seems to offer even more future independence. But in the postwar years, the Soviet Union's emphasis on military and industrial development has enabled it to become one of the most powerful nations on earth, making it unlikely that the centuries-old Ukrainian dream of national sovereignty will be fulfilled in the near future.

So many Ukrainians wished to emigrate in the early decades of the 20th century that the Canadian Pacific Railway opened up offices in the Ukraine.

LEAVING THE VILLAGE BEHIND

Until 1920, when the Russian civil war ended with the Bolshevik victory, 80 percent of the Ukraine's population worked as independent farmers. Families each owned a small plot of land—usually no more than 10 acres—cultivated it themselves, and raised their own livestock. The typical Ukrainian community was a group of small farms, often as many as several thousand, clustered about a village center. Located at this center was a square, which served as meeting place, a market, and a recreational center where villagers would gather for meetings, dances, and musical performances. The center also included communal buildings—churches, a school, stores, the municipal building, the post office, even the home of the local doctor, if the town was fortunate enough to have one.

The characteristic Ukrainian village was a close-knit place. Neighbors assisted one another with their farm labors, pitched in during emergencies, and relaxed together when time permitted. "After a hard day's work in the spring and summer," wrote Miron Dolot, the Ukrainian-American author of *Execution by Hunger: The Hidden Holocaust*, "the young people gathered in neighborhoods at the crossroads and danced, sang, and played long into the night. Families visited relatives and friends, or enjoyed plays, dances, parties, and other kinds of entertainment, all accompanied by much eating and drinking."

The community was the center of the typical Ukrainian farmer's world, and few people perceived themselves as citizens of a larger state or nation. For good reason, most identified themselves exclusively by their region, province, or town. Some Ukrainians never left the village during the course of their lives, and for many, the village was the only life they knew.

Most Ukrainian farmers lived in *xatas*, simple dwellings whose design dates to the beginnings of Ukrainian civilization. Families built their own xata, helped by neighbors. The materials they used were near to hand and easy to obtain: rough-hewn timber, which could be shaped into beams; clay and sand, which could be mixed into plaster (thickened with animal dung) for walls; thatched straw or grass for roofs. Because the single room in the xata had to be used for all the family's daily activities, including cooking and sleeping, much attention was paid to keeping it clean and neat.

Farming had its rewards, but each successive generation found it harder to survive, especially families with a large number of male offspring, each of whom inherited a portion of a plot that had been small to begin with. Few family farms earned a profit sufficient to enable their owners to buy more land, and by the latter decades of the 19th century, the Ukraine's farmers were trapped in a downward spiral of poverty. In 1893, the average farm owned by the 1.6 million peasant families in Galicia—a Ukrainian province then controlled by Austria—was barely 6 acres in area. The crop yield from so meager a plot was insufficient to feed the several

A Ukrainian peasant village near Kiev, photographed in 1918. Most Ukrainians worked their own small farms; the local village was the center of their universe.

families that relied on it let alone to provide a surplus for sale on the marketplace. Meanwhile, a small coterie of Austrian and Russian nobles—less than 5,000 in number—occupied enormous tracts of the choicest land in the Ukraine. The average estate of one of these noblemen totaled 1,700 acres, and the 161 most powerful nobles each owned almost 24,000 acres apiece. The aristocracy imposed high taxes on the smaller landowners, which forced the peasants to relinquish even more of their dwindling acreage.

As the plight of the peasants worsened, they looked for alternative means of earning a living, but few options were available to them in the Ukraine of the late 19th century. Young villagers who migrated to the cities in search of work found little opportunity there. In other parts of Europe, the new technology of the Industrial Revolution had created jobs in urban areas, but the Ukrainian economy would not be modernized for several more decades.

Faced with a life of almost certain poverty, Ukrainian villagers looked to the world outside the borders of their homeland for a way out of their predicament. The place that beckoned most invitingly was North America. In the late 1870s, the first—and largest—wave of Ukrainian immigration to the United States and Canada began. It lasted until the outbreak of World War I in 1914 and brought to the New World an estimated half-million Ukrainians, most of them farmers.

Many of these immigrants left their villages with the hope that they would be able to resume farming in the New World. It was said that in Canada's western provinces and the northern midwest region of the United States large tracts of land were available. Even more enticing was the news that both nations were encouraging settlement. The Homestead Act, for example, passed by the U.S. Congress in 1862, offered 160 acres of free land to anyone willing to cultivate it and live on it for a minimum of 5 years.

To Ukrainian farmers stuck on tiny plots of land, this deal seemed too good to be true. "Good news from

Ukrainian peasant families lived in one-room wooden huts known as xatas. *The xata's roof was made of grass or thatch.*

Ukrainians encountered modern cultural influences even before departing for the New World. This Ukrainian bride and groom eschewed the traditional garb of their homeland in favor of a more western European look.

America reached the village of Bezbrudy . . . about 20 miles east of the city of Lvov," Julia Ann Hurinenko wrote in *Echoing Trails*, a history of Billings County, North Dakota, published in 1979. "[A]nyone 21 years of age or older could get 160 acres of land free from the government in America. All one had to do was to build a house and live on the land for five years and it would become rightfully his. There was . . . much room for expansion in America and a much better way of life. . . . The news sounded unbelievable . . . and very tempting. . . . Anyone owning four or five acres in the Ukraine was considered wealthy. One hundred and sixty acres of free land was unbelievable."

The promise of North America fired the imaginations not only of farmers but also of those who had soured on life in the Ukraine and its attendant hardships. These other immigrants discovered that America offered more than just the possibility of free or cheap land. The prosperous new nation had the very jobs that Ukrainian cities lacked—in factories, mills, mines, and foundries—and the wages were better than in the Ukraine, where an oversupply of workers allowed employers to pay bottom dollar. News of the salaries paid in America—often 10 to 15 times higher than those at home—encouraged many Ukrainians to seek their fortunes in the new land.

Money and land were not the only attractions of North America. In the 1870s, when mass immigration from the Ukraine began, its inhabitants had endured more than 200 years of subjugation at the hands of foreign powers that denied them political and religious freedom. Whether under Russian or Austrian control, Ukrainians faced a compulsory draft into the armed services of what they regarded as an occupying power. The Austrian government required almost every young Ukrainian male to spend two to three years in the Austrian army and forbade them to marry before they had completed this service. America had no such draft, nor did it regulate worship or entrust all political power to a small group of aristocrats. The new nation offered new freedoms, especially to young men, who constituted almost three quarters of all Ukrainian emigrants before World War I.

Like most immigrants to America, the first arrivals from the Ukraine urged their kin to follow them across the ocean by describing their experiences in letters and stories that reached the old country. Some travelers, such as Ivan Pylypiw, took a more direct approach. When Pylypiw and his friend Wasyl Elyniak arrived in Canada in September 1891, they were the first Ukrainian settlers to set foot there. Pylypiw did not stay put for long, however. He quickly returned to the Ukraine, where he sang the praises of his new home to friends and relatives. He urged them to accompany him on his next journey there, but his efforts were halted by the Austrian government, which arrested him, tried him

This 1910 shipping company advertisement touted low rates and the advantages of life in the New World. Some 27,000 Ukrainians emigrated to the United States that year.

An 1874 cartoon depicts emigrants scrambling from under the heeled jackboot of the armies of the European monarchies for the safety of ships bound for America. The prospect of conscription convinced many young Ukrainian men to emigrate.

for sedition, and prevented him from returning to Canada until 1893. Their strategy backfired: The publicity generated by Pylypiw's trial advertised Canada much more effectively than he could have done on his own.

Few Ukrainians left their homeland for the United States during World War I, but with the overthrow of the independent Ukrainian National Republic and the resumption of Russian sovereignty over the area in 1920, emigration resumed. The devastation of World War I, the Russian civil war, and the battle for Ukrainian independence left 20 percent of the farming population homeless and the remainder in dire economic straits. The infant mortality rate rose to 50 percent. The taste of freedom they had enjoyed only made Ukrainians more bitter about the partition of their nation. The first decades of Soviet rule were particularly brutal, and Ukrainians in the western provinces found their Romanian and Czech rulers less tolerant than the Austrians had been. The second wave of Ukrainian immigration lasted from 1920 to 1939; despite the harshness of their lives, particularly under the Soviet regime, many fewer Ukrainians journeyed to the New World during this period than had gone during the first wave. Most of those who did emigrate were from the western provinces. Restrictive Soviet emigration laws kept all but a handful of Ukrainians from leaving the eastern regions.

The Long Journey

The trip to America from the Ukraine was long and hard, and no part of the journey was more difficult than the decision itself—to leave behind family and friends for an unknown future. "A few young men in the village, including my dad, Nick Romanyshyn, made plans to embark for America," wrote Julia Ann Hurinenko in *Echoing Trails*. "It took some time to . . . decide about leaving one's country, friends and relatives—perhaps never to return." Abandoning the safety and familiarity of the village was no easy task, particularly for people who had never once set foot outside their native village. Ahead of them lay the arduous trip across the Atlantic to a world populated by people very different from themselves.

The governments and the nobility of Austria and Russia posed another obstacle: All firmly opposed emigration. The governments feared losing their supply of inductees for the army; the nobles did not want to part with their agricultural labor force. Opposition went beyond disapproval to outright prevention. In March 1877, the Austrian government instructed the Ukrainian clergy to preach against emigration. When sermonizing proved unsuccessful, the government resorted to force. It posted military guards at railroad stations along the Austrian-German border and issued orders to intercept Ukrainians on their way to harbors in Germany, England, and other points of embarkation on the Atlantic. Emigrants had to sneak out of their homeland. "I left my village in Bukovina on the nineteenth of January, 1912," one Ukrainian emigrant remembered much later. "I had to leave at night because I was avoiding conscription into the Austrian army. . . . After making my way through Austria and Germany I eventually got to Antwerp in Belgium."

Money, or the lack of it, was yet another impediment to leaving home. Most Ukrainians found it difficult to raise the cash needed to book passage on ships that sailed to North America. Many mortgaged or sold the family farm; when they still came up short, they were forced to turn to moneylenders, who exacted a high rate of interest. Ukrainians often arrived in the New World broke and in debt.

Those who avoided moneylenders sometimes signed on with shipping companies that had contracted to import labor to North America. These companies were

Wasyl Elyniak (pictured) and his friend Ivan Pylypiw were the first two Ukrainians to emigrate to Canada. Approximately 170,000 of their countrymen followed the pair to Canada before World War I temporarily halted Ukrainian immigration.

Most Ukrainians endured the middle passage to the New World in the crowded steerage sections of steamships—the cheapest accommodation available.

often unscrupulous, and many illiterate Ukrainians, unable to read the contracts they signed—some were even printed in English—were cruelly misled and wound up binding themselves to long periods of labor in return for passage. There were even worse consequences. In 1898, for instance, 365 emigrants were shanghaied to the Hawaiian Islands (at the time a U.S. territory and not yet a state) and reduced to positions of servitude on sugar plantations. They did not win their freedom until several years later, when the Ukrainian press on the American mainland publicized their plight, causing Congress to intervene. No one interceded, however, on the behalf of the thousands of Ukrainians flimflammed by con artists who, claiming to be shipping agents, took the emigrants' money and gave nothing in return.

Once emigrants secured a berth for the transatlantic voyage, they faced a miserable month or so crossing the ocean. Shipboard conditions were abominable. The vessels were packed to the gunwales with Ukrainians and other emigrants from all over Europe drawn by the promise of land and work in the New World. One Ukrainian who immigrated to America as a teenager recalled that when he took a trip across the Atlantic in the 1920s, more than 4,000 people were on board. Most traveled in "steerage," the section of the ship reserved for the lowest-paying passengers. Here filth and disease were rampant, water was in short supply, and food quickly spoiled.

Only a very few Ukrainian immigrants arrived on America's shores with money in their pockets. In 1910, more than 25,000 of the 27,000 immigrants who arrived in the United States from the Ukraine possessed less than $50.00, and the average amount was only $20.42. Not only were these immigrants penniless; they were also, by and large, alone and unwelcome. Many Americans—including immigrants who had arrived from other countries only a generation earlier—felt threatened by this wave of newcomers, and with good reason. Ukrainians and other refugees from economically underdeveloped countries were willing to work for much less than American workers and thus drove down

wages. The new arrivals posed a threat to the fledgling labor movement in the United States; industrialists eager to break strikes and bust labor unions employed the newcomers as scabs, or nonunion workers.

Even those Americans whose livelihoods were not endangered by the immigrants often regarded the Ukrainians with disdain. In 1889, a Canadian newspaper, the *Alberta Tribune*, quoted a French-Canadian priest who remarked, "[a]s for the Galicians [i.e., Ukrainians] I have not met one single person in the whole of the Northwest who is sympathetic towards them. They are, from the [stand]point of civilization, ten times lower than the Indians." This sentiment was shared by other North Americans, many of whom considered eastern Europeans to belong to inferior "racial stock."

Luckily, Ukrainian immigrants also had their advocates. The same year that the French-Canadian clergyman ridiculed them, the Canadian minister of the interior, Clifford Sifton, argued that "our experience of these people teaches us that they are industrious, careful, and law abiding. . . . Their strongest desire is to assimilate with Canadians. . . . They are people who lived in poverty. That is no crime on their part."

Ukrainian immigrants in America faced an uncertain future. Most were unable to read or write and arrived with little or no money.

Ukrainian women pick cabbages on a farm in Manitoba. Ukrainian immigrants found farmland plentiful in Canada's western provinces of Alberta, Saskatchewan, and Manitoba.

No streets paved with gold

Ukrainians first came to North America long before mass migration from their homeland began. The earliest arrival was probably Lawrenty Bohoon, who in 1608 joined the very first permanent English colony in America, at Jamestown, Virginia. It is possible that Bohoon had met the colony's founder, Captain John Smith, in the Ukraine a few years earlier. Smith, who had fought with the Austrians to halt the expansion of the Ottoman Empire, had been captured by the Turks and, according to his account, sent to Constantinople as a gift to the wife of a Turkish pasha. This woman developed a strong affection for Smith and helped him escape through the Ukraine, where he supposedly met Bohoon. In the 1660s, another early colony, founded in Pennsylvania by religious dissidents from the Netherlands and Germany, also included Ukrainians, most likely refugees from religious persecution by the Catholic church in Poland.

Ukrainians did not arrive in force until the early 19th century, when Ukrainians expelled from their homeland by the Russian government helped settle the Russian colonies in Alaska. Located near the Arctic Circle, the Russian settlements found very little land that could be successfully cultivated, and the colonists soon

The settlement at Fort Ross, near the San Francisco Bay, which Ukrainians helped establish in 1812.

grew desperate for food. In 1812, some journeyed south to what is now California and founded the Fort Ross colony near San Francisco Bay. Here the fertile land and temperate climate proved ideal for growing grain and vegetables. The settlement flourished until 1841, when it was bought by John Sutter, the Swedish immigrant whose name became inscribed in American legend in 1848 when gold was discovered on his land.

The roster of early Ukrainian immigrants also included adventurers who came to America to help the fledgling nation during wartime. Ukrainians fought under George Washington's armies in the revolutionary war; the Civil War also included some Ukrainian soldiers.

At least one Ukrainian made a major contribution to American culture before the mass immigration that began in the 1870s. He was the Reverend Agapius Honcharenko, a political refugee who founded, owned, edited, and printed the *Alaska Herald and Svoboda*, which first reached readers on March 1, 1868, less than six months after the U.S. secretary of state, William Seward, arranged to purchase Alaska from Russia.

Suddenly, Alaska's colonists had to learn about American ways, and the *Herald and Svoboda* helped clue them in. It was the first newspaper in the United States printed in Russian, English, and sometimes Ukrainian.

(continued on page 57)

A CELEBRATION OF TRADITION

Overleaf: *Many Ukrainians are grateful for the freedom and opportunity they have found in America.*

The Catholic church has long been the focal point of Ukrainian life in North America, serving as a social and cultural center for the community as well as a place of worship. Congregants at the Ukrainian church in Hunter, New York, participate in various rituals, including the burning of incense (left) and the annual blessing of the fruits (below).

Easter is the holiest time of the year for Ukrainians, who celebrate the holy day by attending church (opposite) *and preparing traditional foods, such as Easter bread, or* pashka (left), *and the elaborately decorated Easter eggs known as* pysanky (below).

Pride in their rich cultural heritage is particularly strong among the members of New York City's Ukrainian community (right). The store operated by the Surma Book and Music Company (above) sells folk instruments, recordings of Ukrainian music, books, periodicals, sheet music, and handicrafts; other shops on Manhattan's Lower East Side (above right) offer traditional Ukrainian garb.

Ukrainian Americans celebrate the memories of their departed kinsfolk and friends on the day of the annual blessing of the graves.

The venerable Reverend Agapius Honcharenko (center, with white beard) holds a copy of the Alaska Herald and Svoboda *while entertaining visitors to his Hayward, California, homestead in the 1880s.*

(continued from page 48)

Although these first Ukrainian Americans, mainly pioneers and adventurers, made individual contributions to the growth of the New World, their life stories do not accurately reflect the experiences of the majority of Ukrainian immigrants who came later.

The Two Waves: 1876–1914 and 1920–39

Neither U.S. nor Canadian immigration records recognized Ukrainian as a separate nationality until 1899, but by then, an estimated 100,000 Ukrainian immigrants had already settled in the United States, with perhaps 20,000 to 30,000 more in Canada. More followed. In 1914 alone—the peak year—almost 37,000 Ukrainians arrived in America. All told, the first wave of immigration (1876–1914) brought more than half a million Ukrainians to North America: Two hundred and fifty-four thousand entered the U.S. between 1899 and 1914, and an estimated 170,000 more settled in Canada from 1891 to 1914.

It was a large but homogenous population. Three quarters were men, and almost 89 percent were between the ages of 14 and 44. The great majority were unskilled and illiterate—refugees from failing farms. An astounding 98 percent of all Ukrainians who came to the United States between 1899 and 1910, including women and children, reported their occupations in the old country

Despite the difficulties of taming a harsh and unyielding land, most Ukrainians who settled in Canada were determined to succeed as farmers. This immigrant family claimed a homestead in Manitoba.

as farm laborers, unskilled laborers, servants, or farmers; others listed no occupation at all. Only 109 Ukrainian immigrants during this period qualified as professionals, and almost half of these were clergymen who came to serve the huge immigrant population.

Many of these immigrants may have planned to stay in North America temporarily—until they saved enough money to return to the old country and buy land. All were bent on improving their lot, and no sacrifice was too great. "You would see it in the early immigrants, in their eyes, in their hands," a second-generation Ukrainian American told Lubomyr K. Luciuk, author of *Ukrainians in the Making*. "Hard work. All they had known was work, but they never regretted coming here."

Eighty-five percent of those who arrived in America settled in Pennsylvania, New York, and New Jersey, states where jobs in mines and factories were readily available. What little homestead land remained in the United States was in the Dakotas, Montana, and the Northwest—a long distance from New York City, Philadelphia, Boston, and other ports of entry. In Canada, by contrast, 94 percent of the Ukrainian population remained farmers, taking advantage of the more plentiful homestead land available in Alberta, Saskatchewan, and Manitoba.

The flow of immigration from the Ukraine was temporarily halted in 1914 by World War I. This conflict also slowed the progress of Ukrainians already living in America, as they became targets of antiforeign sentiment. Some Ukrainian Americans, who had been classified as Austro-Hungarians upon entry, were now viewed as dangerous aliens and interned. (Austria-Hungary and Germany were allied against the United States and other nations during the war.) Canada maintained 24 internment camps, scattered throughout the nation. Those immigrants whose place of birth made them suspect in the eyes of Canada's governmental authorities were uprooted from their homes and spent the war years behind barbed-wire fences. Others who had dreamed of returning to the old country with their savings saw their homeland drastically changed by the war. The immigrants' hope of seeing their native land finally free from foreign tyranny had been dashed with the defeat of the republic and the partition of the Ukraine; few wished to return to a nation ruled, once again, by "outsiders."

In 1920, a second wave of immigration from the Ukraine began, but it was all but halted by restrictions imposed by the U.S. Congress and the government of the Soviet Union. In the United States, a quota imposed in 1924 limited the number of newcomers from each nation to 2 percent of the total population of that group present in 1890. This policy favored groups with older ties to America—people from the British Isles, Scandinavia, and Germany—and effectively barred arrivals from southern and eastern Europe. The quota proved to be more restrictive than it sounded. There were no accurate records of several groups, including Ukrainians, who before 1899 had been listed as natives of Austria, Hungary, Russia, and other countries whose immigration levels had generally been low. As a result, ethnic Ukrainian immigration was severely curtailed, and fewer than 40,000 Ukrainians were admitted into the United States from 1920 to 1939. The extremely restrictive emigration policies instituted by the Soviet Union contributed further to the slowing of Ukrainian immigration at this time.

Most of those who were able to leave the Ukraine headed to Canada. More than 100,000 Ukrainians settled in Canada between 1920 and 1939, almost half of them in the eastern provinces and its largest industrial cities, Montreal and Toronto.

Mining and Industrial Labor

In 1876, when the first Ukrainian immigrants arrived in large numbers, American industrial leaders were mounting an effort to break the nation's growing labor union movement. One means of doing so was to pressure striking workers back into the factory by filling their jobs with foreigners willing to toil for low wages. This required a ready availability of labor, which employers ensured by paying steamship company agents to direct immigrants toward specific mines or factories. In this way, many newcomers from the Ukraine had their first taste of America through work in the coal mines of Pennsylvania and industrial cities of the East Coast, such as Baltimore, Philadelphia, and New York.

Some Ukrainians wanted to continue the agrarian traditions they had known in the old country, but the most desirable homestead lands had been staked out by earlier immigrants. More land was available in Canada, but it was remote and untamed. To survive for the five years required to claim homestead land, settlers needed a reserve of cash larger than the $20 most Ukrainian immigrants brought with them. As a result, most ended up working in mines or factories until they could raise the capital to buy a farm.

One group of immigrants, the Stundinsts—Protestant refugees from the czars' religious persecution—worked in manufacturing industries, mostly textile factories, in Philadelphia for almost 10 years after arriving in America. In 1894, after saving enough money, they bought 10- to 40-acre plots in Virginia and Maryland, cleared the land, and settled down to become poultry farmers.

Almost half of the Ukrainian immigrants who entered the United States during the first wave headed to

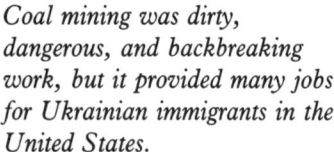

Coal mining was dirty, dangerous, and backbreaking work, but it provided many jobs for Ukrainian immigrants in the United States.

Pennsylvania. Most found work in coal mines in towns such as Shamokin, Shenandoah, Scranton, Olyphant, and Mount Carmel. Many of these immigrants had been induced to settle there by coal companies that wanted cheap labor to replace or intimidate unionizing mine workers. Because they had no money, Ukrainians had little choice but to accept the role of union busters, though it was distasteful and dangerous: The striking miners—many of whom were first- or second-generation Americans—often greeted the Ukrainians with blatant hostility, frequently berating or even assaulting the newcomers who threatened their livelihood. Ukrainians did not wish to act as strikebreakers; indeed, they were no less distressed than other miners by the horrendous conditions of their workplace. Still, they were desperately in need of employment and feared to take any action, such as forming unions, that might get them fired. As newcomers, they seldom felt comfortable rocking the boat. But union organizers did not accept this argument. In their view, the Ukrainians were tools of the mine owners—"scabs"—and crowds of strikers often attacked and hurled stones at Ukrainians who crossed picket lines.

Ukrainian Americans struggled not only with the animosity of their co-workers but also with the strenuous task of mining itself. Most worked 10 or 12 hours a day, 6 days a week, receiving about 60 cents a day for their backbreaking labor. Conditions underground were extremely hazardous and unhealthy. Explosions and cave-ins occurred with alarming frequency, and many mine workers suffered from black lung disease as a result of constant exposure to coal dust.

Most Ukrainian immigrants had sweated for many years as farmers and so were prepared for hard work. They were not prepared, however, for the strict regimentation of industrial labor. Instead of erecting their own xatas, they were forced to live in uniform company houses provided by the mining companies for their employees. And instead of the farming villages of the Ukraine—each with its own history, each a reflection of the generations that had lived there—immigrants in-

Miners' wives hunt for coal atop a slag heap in Hazelton, Pennsylvania, during a coal miners' strike there in the early 1900s that led to the formation of the United Mine Workers labor union.

A sign in Ukrainian advertises the availability of room and board at this house in Yorkton, Saskatchewan, in 1920. Many Ukrainian immigrants earned extra money by renting space in their home.

habited company-built villages devoid of individuality. Often, the only variety in the miners' lives came from the diverse languages and customs of their co-workers.

Most miners were starved for the companionship of the wives and children they had left behind. On the whole, though, wives were often better off in the Ukraine. Those who accompanied their husbands faced a life of unremitting toil. Not only was a woman expected to shop, cook, clean, and wash for her husband and family, but often she also had to perform the same chores for as many as a dozen other men.

These others were boarders. Immigrant couples planning for the arrival of their families acquired extra space to accommodate them. Because they usually could not afford to send for relatives at first, couples raised money by renting lodging to boarders, who were almost always single men. Each paid three to four dollars a month for sleeping space—more if board (daily meals) was included. Boardinghouses—operated by miners and industrial workers alike—were among the first businesses established by Ukrainians in the United States.

American coal companies were not alone in mistreating Ukrainian immigrants. In Canada, railway companies also exploited them as a source of cheap labor. Ukrainians were ideal for such exploitation because poverty had made them "obedient and industrious," in the words of C. W. Speers, an immigration inspector. They quickly became the largest ethnic group working on railroad construction in Canada, where the rail system expanded from 18,000 to 38,000 miles between 1900 and 1918. By providing much of the labor needed on the Canadian Pacific Railway, Ukrainian Americans helped extend the nation's borders from the Atlantic to the Pacific. Other Canadian industries treated Ukrainians similarly. When newcomers arrived, they were often banded together and dispatched wherever cheap labor was needed. In the years following 1907, a great number of Ukrainians were channeled to northern Canada's lumber and mining camps.

Eventually, Ukrainians tired of rude treatment and overcame their initial reluctance to participate in labor actions, especially once they paid off their debts. They then felt secure enough to organize at the workplace and soon joined their co-workers in demanding better on-site conditions, higher wages, and shorter hours. In the summer of 1901, a three-month strike by the Ukrainian Brotherhood of Railway Workers in Canada won formal recognition of the union. The strike was the first successful blow by an ethnic labor organization against industrialists who pitted different ethnic groups against each other in an effort to maintain low wages. In the United States, Ukrainian miners in the hard-coal regions of northeastern Pennsylvania joined with members of other Slavic immigrant groups in major strikes in 1900 and 1902 that helped establish the United Mine Workers of America.

Members of the second wave of Ukrainian immigration continued to find work primarily in mining and industry. As late as 1935, near the end of the second wave, almost 90 percent of all Americans born in the Ukraine worked here as miners or industrial workers. A few Ukrainians, especially in urban ethnic neighborhoods, owned stores or restaurants or operated businesses—as tailors, barbers, and printers—but the vast majority of those not employed in mines or factories lived and worked on farms.

Canada more than doubled its total railway mileage between 1900 and 1918. Ukrainian Americans provided much of the necessary labor.

Land in Canada and the Northwest

Because earlier immigrants had already settled the best land available under the Homestead Act, Ukrainian farmers had to consider other means of obtaining property for farming. One option was to buy developed farms, but this required much more capital than most Ukrainian Americans were capable of raising. A second option was to rent land, which went against the grain of a people long used to owning their own farms. A third was to hire themselves out as laborers to other farmers, which—again—did not sit well with Ukrainians. The final option for prospective farmers was to venture into the western lands where property was still available under the American and Canadian homestead acts. Many Ukrainians set out for North Dakota and Montana or the provinces of Alberta, Saskatchewan, and Manitoba.

The land in these areas was often wild, but Ukrainian immigrants were equipped to tame it. In the western Ukraine, where most of these immigrants had originally farmed, barren or rocky soil characterized much of the terrain. As a result, Ukrainian homesteaders were used to the arduous tasks—clearing land, unearthing rocks, tilling difficult soil—necessary to settle the frontier.

Many newcomers to western Canada discovered that they faced weeks and even months of labor clearing the soil before they could plant crops.

In about 1896, the first group of Ukrainian-American farmers arrived in North Dakota, where the climate and soil reminded many of them of the steppes of the Ukraine. They had their work cut out for them, however. The land needed to be cleared of trees, rocks, and stones. Immigrants needed to erect makeshift shelters until they had built replicas of the xatas they had known in the old country. Their meals were poor and drab. Staples included beans cooked in a soup or mashed with garlic and served over bread. Occasionally, a more established farmer might offer a new homesteader flour or bacon, the drippings of which could be used as butter. There was more variety in their beverages. Crops could be made into beer, whiskey, wine, and root beer, and wild fruit could be squeezed into juices.

The lean times lasted several years, but the land was fertile, and most of the farmers were able to make a go of it. The pioneers sent boastful letters to friends and relatives in Canada, in other parts of the United States, and in the Ukraine. These accounts had such a powerful effect that within 15 years the Ukrainian-American population in the Dakotas reached 8,000.

In the early 20th century, hardy Ukrainian pioneers also settled successfully in many other prairie states, as well as in the central Canadian provinces. In Wisconsin, the only low-priced land available to Ukrainian settlers was in the north, where forests had recently stood. The land—pocked with stumps and dense with underbrush—needed to be cleared, and years passed before it yielded even moderately prosperous harvests. In Michigan, Ukrainian farmers bought undeveloped wooded land that took years of struggle to successfully convert into fruit and corn farms. In Canada, Ukrainian immigrants established settlements throughout the northern regions of Saskatchewan, Alberta, and Manitoba.

All these Ukrainian-American farmers sacrificed comfort, convenience, and ease, but for many the struggle itself and the beauty of the land was rewarding.

"Like all men who work the land [my father] found himself subject to the fickleness of the prairie weather," wrote Beverly Palaniuk, a third-generation Ukrainian American born in North Dakota, in *Echoing Trails*. "A hailstorm upon golden wheat could and often did make [him] cry. But in the spring the steady hiss of rain hitting the freshly sown field caused Dad to roam from window to window before finally standing on the front steps, breathing in the cool revitalized air and saying, 'Agnes, Agnes, come smell the rain.'"

World War I: The Homefront

The progress made by many of these settlers halted during World War I. Within months of the outbreak of war, suspicion and mistrust of "foreigners" arose throughout Canada. The victims were most often unskilled laborers and the unemployed. In 1914, an emergency act of the Canadian government called for measures to be taken against foreigners, and a total of 8,759 men, 81 women, and 156 children—all "enemy aliens"—were removed from their homes and sent to one of Canada's two dozen internment camps, where they were forced to perform industrial labor related to the war effort. Almost 6,000 of those imprisoned were classified as Austro-Hungarians, a misnomer in many cases because the total included Ukrainians from Galicia and Bukovina, provinces that happened to be controlled by the Austro-Hungarian Empire. Canadian authorities could not be bothered, however, with such distinctions. As a result, a majority of those labeled "Austro-Hungarians" and incarcerated were actually Ukrainians. Many of the Ukrainian men who escaped internment enlisted in the Commonwealth army. More than 10,000 Ukrainians fought for Canada, and at least one—Corporal Philip Konowal—received the Victoria Cross, the British Empire's highest decoration for valor. Another 30,000 men of Ukrainian descent served in the U.S. armed forces. Yet this patriotism was ignored by the Canadian government. In 1917, it stripped Ukrainians of the right to vote and revoked the citizenship of any "foreigners" naturalized after 1902.

Ukrainian-language newspapers reacted to the incarceration program and the abolition of immigrants' rights with anger, indignation, and sorrow. "The Ukrainians were invited to Canada and promised liberty and a kind of paradise," the *Canadian Ruthenian* lamented in 1918. "Instead . . . they found woods and rocks, which had to be cut down to make the land fit to work on. They were given farms far from the railroads, which they so much helped in building—but still they worked hard . . . and came to love Canada. But . . . liberty did not last long. First they were called 'Galicians' in mockery. Secondly, preachers were sent amongst them, as if they were savages, to preach Protestantism. And thirdly, they were deprived of the right to elect their representatives in Parliament. They are now uncertain about their future in Canada." Such protests were cut short when the government suppressed the publication of the newspapers they appeared in.

Canadian hysteria against foreigners eased somewhat as the war dragged on and the country suffered a labor shortage. Many imprisoned Ukrainians were paroled and forced to work either in remote mining and timber camps in northern Canada or in munitions factories and other war industries in the east. By the time the Canadian Parliament discontinued its internment program in 1918, severe damage had already been done. The blatant discrimination Ukrainian immigrants suffered broke the spirits of many of them, and the unjust treatment heaped upon the Ukrainians during the war shattered many of their hopes for a better life in the New World.

World War I brought an outburst of xenophobia in Canada that led to the internment of more than 8,000 "enemy aliens." Many Ukrainians were misclassified as Austro-Hungarians and suffered imprisonment as a result.

Ukrainian Americans gather to celebrate the completion of their church in Gorham, North Dakota, in 1912. Religion was a unifying element in Ukrainian-immigrant communities.

A SOCIETY WITHIN A SOCIETY

During the first decades of the 1900s, the Ukrainians struggled for acceptance within their adopted countries in North America. The prejudice they encountered often disheartened them, but Ukrainians united in the face of intolerance and gained a new appreciation and understanding of their ethnic identity. Many immigrants from the Ukraine had lacked any cultural consciousness prior to their emigration. This was especially true of the first wave of Ukrainian immigrants, many of whom classified themselves not as "Ukrainian" but as "Ruthenian"—a term derived from the word "Rusins," referring to the ancient Rus tribe. Some newcomers of this era simply called themselves Russians or Austrians, depending on which country had issued their passports. In truth, the peasants who composed the first wave of immigrants had little time or inclination to speculate about questions of Ukrainian nationality because they were preoccupied with the daily struggle for survival. Few of these poor farmers had ever left their village before emigrating. They knew almost nothing of the world beyond their small towns and therefore identified themselves by village or by province: For example, those from the region of Galicia called themselves "Galicians." These regional loyalties sometimes caused strife within Old

Many individuals among the first wave of Ukrainian immigration did not perceive of themselves as possessing a distinct national identity. This young woman, photographed at Ellis Island in 1906, was classified as Ruthenian rather than Ukrainian.

World Ukrainian settlements. Galicians, Bukovinans, and Ruthenians, for example, all regarded each other as foreigners and had little sense of a common heritage or a shared culture.

For most Ukrainian Americans who came to America before World War I, the idea of a national identity became important only after immigration. Once they found themselves surrounded by a sea of strangers, they latched on to one another, and the regional differences that had once chafed now seemed insignificant. In making friends with people who shared the same ancestry—and often the same jobs and neighborhoods—Ukrainian Americans began to forge a new identity together in tight-knit mining villages and urban communities. Far from their homeland, Ukrainians immersed themselves in an extended family of other immigrants from the Ukraine, thereby gaining a sense of belonging in an alien land.

The second wave of Ukrainian immigrants differed from their predecessors in their conception of what it meant to be Ukrainian. Whereas the earlier arrivals gradually attained an identity as Ukrainians, the postwar immigrants arrived in North America as fervent patriots. The latter group had witnessed the rise of nationalism within their homeland and associated their own heritage with the crusade for Ukrainian liberation and the founding of the Ukrainian National Republic. They regarded a public declaration of their Ukrainian identity as a political act and vowed to work in the New World to advance the cause of a free Ukraine.

Despite these fundamental differences, both waves of immigrants shared a common desire to preserve and express their culture and history within the greater American society. One of the first things Ukrainian immigrants did after finding a means of making a living was to establish educational and political organizations, found economical cooperative institutions, publish newspapers in both English and their native tongue, and—perhaps most importantly—construct churches that would become the center of Ukrainian life in North America.

Music helped Ukrainian immigrants preserve their culture as well as keep their memories of the homeland alive.

Ukrainian Churches

The church served as more than a place of worship in Ukrainian communities. Often the first buildings erected in a Ukrainian neighborhood, community churches housed social and cultural centers for immigrants and their families. Churches acted as community libraries, reading rooms, and Sunday schools; they provided performance space for concerts and amateur plays, rehearsal space for choruses, orchestras and bands, and meeting rooms for various ethnic associations and organizations.

These many services fell under the domain of the clergy. Ukrainian priests performed a variety of services for their parishioners: They sponsored Ukrainian performance groups, edited and printed the first newspapers, organized Ukrainian fraternal societies, and generally eased the transition from the Old World to the New. Indeed, the clergy played a central role in the successful adjustment of Ukrainians to life in the United States and Canada.

Ukrainian Catholics

But Ukrainians did not always have a clergy to whom they could turn. Because the first groups of Ukrainian immigrants lacked their own priests, they often attended services in the churches of other eastern European rites—particularly the Roman Catholic churches

Shenandoah, Pennsylvania, was the site of the first Ukrainian Catholic parish in the United States. Pictured is the second St. Michael's Ukrainian Catholic Church, which was built there in 1908.

attended by Poles. But most Ukrainian Americans felt distinctly uncomfortable attending Polish-American Catholic churches. Despite their shared Slavic ancestry, Ukrainians and Poles regarded one another with deep-seated hostility and antagonism. Ukrainian immigrants blamed their homeland's oppression on Poland and denounced the Poles as enemies of a free Ukraine.

The Ukrainians were alienated, too, by the Latin liturgy practiced by the Poles—a distinct contrast to the Old Slavonic mass preferred by Ukrainian Catholics. Although they attended church regularly, most Ukrainians took little comfort in the rites and rituals of the Catholic church as practiced by Polish Americans. They resolved to organize and construct uniquely Ukrainian places of worship where they could preserve the religious traditions of the old country. These Old World practices included the celebration of holidays according to the Julian calendar rather than the Gregorian calendar commonly used by the Roman Catholic church. Ukrainians also deviated from western Catholics in the Ukrainians' acceptance of married priests.

The First Ukrainian Parish

In the 1880s, a group of Ukrainian Catholics in Shenandoah, Pennsylvania, brought the Ukrainian church to America. They sent an appeal to the head of the Catholic church in Galicia, Cardinal Sembratovich, asking him to assign a Ukrainian priest to their parish. In response to that request, the Reverend John Volansky, a young priest, arrived in Shenandoah in 1884, accompanied by his wife.

Roman Catholic officials and Volansky's immediate superior, the bishop of Philadelphia, condemned the "heresy" of a married priest and demanded that the pope recall Volansky at once. Volansky, pointing out that the pope had recognized a married Ukrainian clergy since 1596, ignored the bishop's insistence that he leave and settled in Shenandoah to begin his work.

Volansky earned a reputation as a tireless organizer and religious leader. In addition to fulfilling his priestly duties, he oversaw construction of the first Ukrainian churches in America, traveling throughout the United States to minister to all Ukrainian Americans. Volansky also published the first Ukrainian-language newspaper—called *Ameryka*—in the United States, helped organize the first Ukrainian benevolent association, choir, and dramatic club, and established nonprofit cooperative stores in the mining communities. He also supported the unionization of mine workers in the late 1880s. Despite Volansky's many good works, he met with criticism from Pennsylvania's Roman Catholic hierarchy, which demanded he leave the country. Finally, under pressure from the Vatican, Volansky's superiors in the old country recalled him to the Ukraine in 1889.

Throughout the 19th century, Ukrainian Catholics struggled with the American hierarchy of the Roman Catholic church over their right to practice eastern rites within the church. In 1891, this conflict came to a head when the Reverend Alex Toth, a Ukrainian priest in Minneapolis, left the Catholic church after the bishop of St. Paul refused to accept him into his diocese. Toth converted to the Russian Orthodox church and started a campaign to persuade other Ukrainians that only the Orthodox church would allow them to preserve their ethnic heritage.

Although Toth achieved some degree of success in his efforts, most Ukrainian Catholics continued to press America's Catholic hierarchy for the right to practice their own form of worship within the church. In 1902, a convention of Ukrainian Catholic parishes, meeting in Pennsylvania, demanded that the Vatican create a separate Catholic diocese for Ukrainian Americans. Although the pope did not respond immediately, by 1907 the Ukrainian Catholic church in America had welcomed its first bishop, Stephen Soter Ortynsky.

Bishop Ortynsky organized the new Ukrainian diocese and unified the clergy, but he soon discovered

The Reverend John Volansky was dispatched from the Ukraine to Shenandoah, Pennsylvania, in 1884 to administer to Ukrainian Catholics there. It was Volansky who founded St. Michael's Ukrainian Catholic Church.

The Reverend Alex Toth, a Russian Orthodox priest, blesses Easter baskets filled with pysanky *(ornately decorated Easter eggs) outside St. Mary's Church in Minneapolis, Minnesota.*

that he did not have the same freedom enjoyed by other bishops within the Catholic church because he served under the jurisdiction of a Roman Catholic bishop. Ukrainian Catholics continued to pressure the Vatican to grant Ortynsky the authority given to other Catholic bishops in the United States. In 1913, the pope honored these requests, declaring the Ukrainian Catholic parishes a separate administrative unit subject only to the Vatican. This decree granted Bishop Ortynsky authority over more than 200 Ukrainian Catholic parishes in the United States. The climate of increasing tolerance enabled Ukrainian Catholics to preserve their unique rites and traditions and to expand church membership to 250,000 by the mid-1980s.

During the 20th century, the church made only one major concession to papal authority. Ukrainians from Galicia and those from Ruthenia had traditionally established separate congregations. In 1924, church authorities formalized this split by assigning Ukrainians two bishops to succeed Bishop Ortynsky, one for the Galicians and one for the Ruthenians. Several years later Galician bishop Konstantin Bohachovsky and Ruthenian bishop Wasyl Takach received a papal mandate decreeing that in the future Ukrainian Catholic priests in America would not be permitted to marry. Despite the opposition of many Ukrainian-American priests, both bishops supported the directive. As a result, many Catholic priests during this period defected to the newly founded Ukrainian Orthodox church.

Orthodox and Protestant Ukrainians

In 1915, 30 years after the first Ukrainian Catholic church was built in Shenandoah, a group of Orthodox Ukrainians founded the independent Ukrainian People's church in Chicago. Until then, most Eastern Orthodox Ukrainians had attended Russian Orthodox services. Ukrainian Orthodoxy remained linked to Russian Orthodoxy in America for many years, just as it had in the Ukraine. Few parishioners even remembered a self-governing Ukrainian Orthodox church in the old country, because the Russian Orthodox church had officially absorbed it in the mid-19th century.

The Ukrainian People's church encouraged believers in Ukrainian Orthodoxy to break away from the Russian church, and the movement toward autonomous Ukrainian Orthodox churches grew quickly. In 1920, a convention of Orthodox Ukrainians announced a plan to join the Galician and Ruthenian branches of the rite by establishing the Ukrainian Orthodox Church of America. In 1928, Ukrainian Catholics protested the pope's prohibition of married clergy by founding the Ukrainian Orthodox church in America.

Like the Orthodox Ukrainians, Ukrainian-American Protestants longed to freely practice their beliefs. Although Ukrainian Baptists began immigrating as early as 1890, the first Ukrainian Baptist congregation was not founded until 1905, in Scranton, Pennsylvania. In 1909, the first Ukrainian Presbyterian parish, in Newark, New Jersey, was established. Ukrainian Protestants began consolidating various parishes in the 1920s. In 1922, the Union of Ukrainian Evangelical Baptist Churches was formed for this purpose. After the merger, Ukrainian Protestant denominations saw little growth until 1950, when new congregations were founded in large cities from Philadelphia to Los Angeles.

The Reverend Soter Ortynsky became the first Ukrainian Catholic bishop in the United States in 1907.

Ukrainian Community Organizations

Ukrainian churches in the United States served as more than houses of worship; they insured the preservation

A SOCIETY WITHIN A SOCIETY

of Ukrainian culture and national identity through the founding of a variety of Ukrainian-American organizations and associations. In 1885, the first Ukrainian organization founded in America—the Reverend Volansky's St. Nicholas Brotherhood—addressed one of the most pressing concerns of the early Ukrainian immigrants: the effect of poverty on their families. The brotherhood, which offered death benefits (life insurance) to its members' families, lasted less than 10 years, but its many successors have benefitted thousands of Ukrainian immigrants and their families.

Perhaps the most significant function performed by the many Ukrainian benevolent associations that succeeded the St. Nicholas Brotherhood has been the establishment of special funds, accumulated through minimal monthly contributions by their members. These funds were used to finance the publication of Ukrainian newspapers, almanacs, and books and to provide benefits for orphans, the sick, and the needy. After World War I, benevolent organizations also tapped these funds to send aid to philanthropic institutions and indigent persons in the Ukraine. The most well known of these groups, the Ukrainian National Association (UNA), was founded in Shamokin, Pennsylvania, in 1894. It offered its members insurance and also provided money to support cultural, social, and recreational activities. As the UNA—which boasted a membership of 75,000 in 1987—approaches its centennial celebration, it stands as the oldest and largest of the surviving Ukrainian benevolent associations.

The first Ukrainian women's organizations were established in 1897. Although many vanished quickly, the Ukrainian National Women's League of America (UNWLA), founded in 1925 in Philadelphia, was still active in the mid-1980s and claimed more than 8,000 members. In addition to providing assistance to the needy, the UNWLA has played a significant role in preserving Ukrainian traditions and culture, raising funds to found and sustain Ukrainian schools and sponsoring concerts and art exhibits. In 1976 the UNWLA founded the Ukrainian Museum in New York City "to

In 1912 the executive officers of the Ukrainian National Association, one of the most important Ukrainian-American organizations, and the editorial staff of the Ukrainian-language daily newspaper Svoboda met to discuss raising funds for the support of education in the Ukraine.

acquire, preserve, exhibit, and interpret articles of artistic, historical, and scientific value related to Ukrainian life and culture."

In 1902, Ukrainians began founding clubs for the community's young people. At first these organizations provided little but physical recreation for Ukrainian children, but in the 1920s, the focus of these groups became increasingly cultural. Fearful that as their children became assimilated the traditions of the homeland would be lost, Ukrainian-American parents used these after-school and weekend programs to teach the younger generation about the language, history, and heritage of the old country.

Young Ukrainians were especially attracted to societies dedicated to the preservation and performance of Ukrainian folk music and dancing. Perhaps the most popular of all these groups was the Ukrainian Youth

League of North America, founded during the 1930s, which offered courses in Ukrainian culture and athletics. That decade also witnessed the proliferation of more politically oriented youth groups, such as the Ukrainian National Youth Federation (UNYF). Founded to promote a free Ukraine, the UNYF was still in existence in the 1980s.

Of course, Ukrainian youth organizations were not the only groups created to further political causes. Most youth societies had adult counterparts, such as the Organization for the Rebirth of the Ukraine, founded after the Soviet Union crushed the Ukrainian National Republic. Although some of the earliest political organizations supported socialism—probably in reaction to the oppressions of the Austro-Hungarian and the Russian aristocracies—the majority espoused independent Ukrainian nationalism. Dr. Kyrylo Trylovsky, an administrator for the Ukrainian Aid Association, expressed the prevailing political sentiments of many Ukrainian Americans of the day when he wrote in the organization's 1925 almanac, "Immigration is significant to the extent it helps the Native Land to its cultural, economical, and primarily, its political freedom."

The Ukrainian Press

Both churches and social organizations exercised great influence in shaping the political and social views of the Ukrainian community. Toward the end of the 19th century, these two forces were joined by a third: the Ukrainian-American press. On August 15, 1886, Reverend Volansky launched *Ameryka*, the first Ukrainian-American newspaper in North America. The bimonthly publication, written in Ukrainian, cost subscribers just two dollars annually. *Ameryka* folded within four years of its first edition, but it provided a model for many other periodicals including *Svoboda*, printed by the Ukrainian National Association. Established in 1894, *Svoboda* was still being published in the 1980s.

The inaugural issue of Ameryka, *the first Ukrainian-language newspaper, appeared in 1886. Founded by the Reverend John Volansky,* Ameryka *continued publishing until 1890.*

The Ukrainian press overcame many obstacles in order to publish in North America. Typeface in the Cyrillic alphabet was difficult to obtain outside of Europe, and newspapers could often afford only a staff of one to edit all the articles in each issue. Because Ukrainian-American newspapers lacked a sound financial base and could generate little income from selling advertisements—problems common to foreign periodicals—they were forced to rely on community organizations and churches for their funding. As late as the 1980s, churches and community organizations, rather than individuals or independent companies, printed and circulated the 2 daily papers, 50 weeklies, and handful of magazines and journals that make up the Ukrainian-American press. Until the decades following World War II, their readership was limited by the high rate of illiteracy among Ukrainian-American adults.

Despite these problems, Ukrainian periodicals proliferated between the 1880s and the 1930s. Seventy-nine different newspapers began publishing during that period. Although 52 of them folded within several years, the Ukrainian-language press succeeded in keeping its readers (both literate Ukrainians and the many who listened as others read to them) informed about events in their new home and in Europe, especially in the old country.

Folk Art: Music, Dance, and Crafts

Beginning in the 1920s, Ukrainian Americans became actively concerned with the preservation of Ukrainian folk culture. Before this time, Ukrainian music and

Young members of a Ukrainian folk ballet company in Minneapolis, Minnesota. Ukrainian folk dancing proved extremely popular in the United States and Canada during the 1920s and 1930s.

dance had been confined to private gatherings, such as weddings or family celebrations. But in the mid-1920s, Vasyl Avramenko brought formal techniques of choreography to this spontaneous dance form. He introduced Ukrainian national dance to the stage, first in Canada and then in the United States, popularizing an ethnic art previously unknown outside the Ukrainian community. Avramenko's performances met with such enthusiasm that he began offering lessons in Ukrainian dance around North America. By 1940, close to 10,000 children of Ukrainian immigrants had taken Ukrainian dance courses taught by Avramenko or his followers.

During the 1920s and 1930s, the popularity of Ukrainian national dance was rivaled by that of the region's folk music. The homeland's musical traditions were preserved by individuals and church choirs, but the hymns and traditional melodies of the old country remained unknown to those outside the Ukrainian community until 1921, when Alexander Koshetz and the Ukrainian National Chorus traveled from Europe to the United States for concert engagements across the country. While on tour, the chorus learned that the Ukraine had fallen to the Soviets and decided to remain in America rather than return home to face the new regime.

Koshetz's vibrant renditions of Ukrainian songs won a large following for the music of his homeland and generated enough interest in Ukrainian music to spawn a small record industry. Albums were produced featuring many traditional Ukrainian folk songs, including hundreds of Christmas carols, songs for the spring and Easter season, harvest songs, love songs, and wedding songs that reflected the culture of Ukrainian peasants. In the 1930s, these peasant songs became so popular that the Surma Book and Music Company, which still exists in New York City, sponsored weekly radio programs of Ukrainian music, broadcast over 18 different stations.

Ukrainian Americans have also taken great care to preserve crafts native to their homeland. In America,

Such traditional Ukrainian images as the trident and eight-pointed star appear on the brilliantly colored Easter eggs known as pysanky.

the best known of these traditional crafts is the creation of elaborately patterned *pysanky*, or Easter eggs. The Ukrainian tradition of dyeing Easter eggs dates back to pre-Christian Kievan Russia, when tribes conducted fertility rituals to welcome the arrival of spring. These ancient origins are reflected in the traditional Ukrainian images—such as tridents and eight-pointed stars—that appear on the intricately designed eggs. Other Ukrainian crafts still practiced in the New World include embroidery, wood carving, weaving, and ceramics. One Ukrainian American commented on the value of preserving his people's traditional heritage in America: "We received a cherished gift from our parents. They taught us to communicate in Ukrainian. They taught us to appreciate our culture. It is our tradition to preserve the art of Ukrainian Easter egg dyeing. These are precious gifts we will never forget."

Holidays

Ukrainian Americans maintained many traditions of the old country in their celebration of holidays. Most immigrants observed not only religious holidays, but Ukrainian national holidays as well. Many of those who emigrated from the western Ukraine celebrated the First of November as a day of national independence, much as Americans observe the Fourth of July. Foreign-born Ukrainian Americans also remembered Shevchenko Day, in commemoration of the 1814 birth of the Ukraine's most revered poet. Ukrainian Americans usually celebrated these holidays by attending special church services followed by short speeches and musical performances.

Old country traditions dictated the observance of religious holidays as well, particularly among first- and second-generation immigrant families. Christmas celebrations began with a meatless Christmas Eve supper consisting of many courses. The lighthearted spirit of Christmas contrasted with the solemnity of the next great event on the Ukrainian church calendar, Lent—the 40-day period of penitence and fasting between Ash Wednesday and Easter. Ukrainian Americans have traditionally commemorated Easter—the holiest time of the year for them—by staging *Haivki*, Ukrainian Easter games. Usually held on church grounds, Haivki consist of singing, folk dances, and contests. Josephine Evoniuk, a third-generation Ukrainian American, wrote fondly of this holiday in *Echoing Trails*:

> Easter was a special time in our house. An Easter basket was prepared on Holy Saturday. In the basket were *pashka* (Easter bread), *yayerechki* (eggs), home-cured *shunka* (ham), *secar* (cheese), *hrin* (beets and horseradish), *maslo* (butter), and *kolbasa* (homemade sausage).... On Easter Sunday, after the celebration of the Divine Liturgy and the glorious singing ... came the blessing of the food. The baskets were placed in a circle formation with a lighted candle placed in each basket. The flickering lights added to the impressive beauty of the prayers and songs. The baskets represent a humble offering brought to the resurrected Christ. The baskets are taken home where the families gather for an early morning meal. The blessed food terminates the lenten feast.

The observance of traditional Ukrainian celebrations of the holidays—like the practice of old country folk arts—has maintained the Ukrainian cultural heritage in the United States and Canada. By working together, Ukrainian individuals and institutions in America have held on to their ethnic identity, despite the strong Americanizing influence of the "melting pot" in which they live.

A newly arrived Ukrainian immigrant family at the headquarters of the United Ukrainian-American Relief Committee (UUARC) in 1950.

A DIFFERENT KIND OF IMMIGRANT

The end of World War II brought a different kind of Ukrainian immigrant to America. Unlike previous arrivals, these newcomers did not come in search primarily of economic prosperity, although they did seek a better life. More than 250,000 Ukrainians had been displaced by the war, either driven out of their homeland by Nazi troops or loaded onto boxcars and sent to German labor camps. When Germany surrendered to the Allies in 1945, these Ukrainians gained their release.

Few wanted to go home—not after 25 years of Soviet oppression, including the famine of 1932–33. Among the ranks of the uprooted Ukrainians were intellectuals, skilled workers, and professionals who had been imprisoned by the Poles before the war for advocating the liberation of Ukrainian territories under Polish rule. "After the war was over," wrote Miron Dolot in *Execution by Hunger*, "knowing that all Soviet prisoners of war were declared deserters and traitors by Stalin's order and faced the firing squad, and because of my desire to live in the free world, I decided to stay in West Germany as a displaced person, and later on I emigrated to the United States where I found my new home."

These displaced persons resettled in countries willing to accept them. By 1950, more than 90 percent of the Ukrainians who had been in displaced-persons

Members of the UUARC welcome another immigrant family to New York City in 1949. In the years immediately following World War II more than 100,000 Ukrainians displaced by the war found new homes in North America.

camps had found new homes, almost half of them in the United States and Canada. Many were assisted by the United Ukrainian-American Relief Committee, the Ukrainian Canadian Relief Fund, and dozens of other volunteer agencies. The United States admitted 85,000 Ukrainian immigrants after World War II. Canada, which had enlisted 40,000 Ukrainian Canadians in its armed services during the war, welcomed 40,000 more Ukrainians as new immigrants in the years following the war. With the exception of fewer than 20,000 Ukrainians who arrived after first attempting to resettle in other countries, mostly in Europe, the flow of Ukrainian immigrants to America all but ended after 1955.

New Immigrants

This final wave brought a new kind of Ukrainian immigrant to America. A large proportion were from urban areas and were well educated. Many had received college degrees, and a large number were doctors, lawyers, engineers, and other professionals. Ukrainian writers, artists, professors, and teachers also came to America at this time.

Worldly as these newcomers were, many felt the same trauma their forebears had experienced when they contemplated starting their lives anew outside their homeland. "My mother and my brother," Miron Dolot recalled, "who suffered with me, who shared with me the last morsel of food, and to whom I owe my survival, remained in the village. They had no other choice but to continue working on the collective farm. World War II separated us and what happened to them afterwards I don't know."

But in addition to their schooling, the postwar arrivals had another advantage over earlier immigrants: They had some idea of what to expect. From correspondence with immigrants already living in America, they knew that the streets in the New World were not paved with gold and that a struggle awaited them. Immigrant status still seemed preferable to the lives they had known as displaced persons and political refugees. They readily accepted their new lot and dedicated themselves to making a contribution to the growth of their adopted homeland.

Most of the Ukrainians who came to America after the war settled in eastern and midwestern urban centers, where they found long-established communities of their countrymen. Many of the older immigrants had financed their compatriots' journey from the homeland, and they welcomed the new arrivals into their homes, often providing them with shelter until they could find apartments and jobs. The older generation also shared their own experiences as strangers in a new land, thereby easing the newcomers' adjustment to American customs.

The postwar refugees owed much to the earlier generation of immigrants, and they repaid the debt by revitalizing ethnic awareness in the Ukrainian-American community. War and displacement had instilled a passionate pride in their national identity. They were appalled by the apathy of Ukrainian political organizations in America, particularly by the lack of interest in freeing the Ukraine from Soviet domination, an issue that was of burning importance to postwar immigrants.

Displaced persons who came to the United States after World War II were often processed by immigration officials aboard the ocean liners that carried them to their new land.

More than 18,000 Ukrainian Americans gathered at the Washington Monument on October 2, 1983, to commemorate the great famine of the 1930s. Those Ukrainians who came to America after either of the two world wars tended to be more politically active than the first wave of immigrants.

Such political concerns led postwar immigrants to reshape and revitalize Ukrainian-American organizations. In the opinion of some newcomers, liberating the Ukraine was of greater importance than preserving folk culture. Others were alarmed by the socialist and communist elements still present in some Ukrainian-American organizations. Loudly asserting that the members of any group advocating a socialist Ukraine no longer understood the Ukrainian cause and the damage done to it by the Soviet Union, they set about dismantling the liberal wings of established Ukrainian organizations.

The new immigrants also created their own organizations, designed to put forward their visions of what it meant to be a Ukrainian. In 1946, the New York–based Organization for the Defense of the Four Freedoms began to use publications and protests to further the cause of Ukrainian freedom. North of the border, the Canadian League for Ukraine's Liberation, established in 1949, became a prominent advocate of

an independent and sovereign Ukraine. The Association of Former Ukrainian Political Prisoners brought together Ukrainians who had suffered from Soviet, Polish, or Nazi imprisonment and were committed to securing an independent Ukrainian nation.

Politically minded youth groups also appeared after World War II. The Ukrainian Youth Association of America and Plast, the Ukrainian scouting organization, were both founded in 1950. Both organizations operated summer camps and sponsored various recreational and cultural activities in Ukrainian communities throughout America. The growing number of Ukrainian-American college students led to the foundation of the Federation of Ukrainian Student Organizations of America in 1953. All these organizations emphasized cultural and national pride and a certain degree of political activism.

Not all new Ukrainian-American organizations had political agendas. Spurred by the arrival of a better-educated class of immigrants, professional associations arose. The first had been founded during Ukrainian week at the Chicago World's Fair in 1933, but it had suffered from a lack of funds and members. After the war, however, many groups thrived, including the Ukrainian Engineers Society, the Ukrainian Medical Association of North America, the Ukrainian Lawyers Organization, and the Ukrainian Artists Association. Most of these professional societies publish annual or quarterly professional journals.

Postwar Ukrainian organizations also established new scholarly organizations dedicated to research and to the publication of information on the Ukraine. The most prominent of these are the Shevchenko Scientific Society and the Ukrainian Academy of Arts and Sciences. Both maintain libraries and archives of Ukrainian material and sponsor conferences and lectures on Ukrainian issues.

Clothed in the traditional costume of their homeland, Ukrainian-American girls dance along New York City's Fifth Avenue in front of the New York Public Library.

PRESERVATION VERSUS ASSIMILATION

Like all immigrants, Ukrainian Americans had to make many adjustments in confronting the unfamiliar customs of American life. The most difficult by far was learning the English language. Few of the Ukrainians who arrived in North America understood a word of English. In fact, 60 percent of those who came before 1914 could not read or write in any language, and even the literate had very little formal schooling.

Ukrainian-American communities began to fight illiteracy almost immediately. As early as the 1880s, Ukrainian churches established reading rooms and libraries and sponsored classes that taught adults how to read and write in both Ukrainian and English. Learning two alphabets and two written languages was an intimidating prospect, and prior to the 20th century, many Ukrainian immigrants felt most comfortable with the spoken tongue of the old country.

The next generation—those born in North America—picked up English quickly and easily. Their training ground was public school. By the time most Ukrainian Americans had graduated from high school (as most did), they had become thoroughly versed in the English language and had even started teaching it to their parents.

91

Out of this fluency grew conflict. Older Ukrainians recognized that their children needed to learn English, the language of their adopted homeland, but they feared that if the younger generation abandoned the Ukrainian language, they would also forsake their heritage. Even before the 20th century, immigrants took steps to use education to keep their culture alive. In 1893, the Ukrainian Catholic church in Shamokin, Pennsylvania, founded the first Ukrainian parish school in America. It employed the services of the priest and the cantor—leader of the church's choral groups—to instruct children in Ukrainian language and culture. Other communities gradually established their own parish schools. Still, it took almost 30 years for these schools to become fixtures in Ukrainian-American communities. By that time, many second- and even third-generation Americans had grown up with no formal schooling in the Ukrainian language. *Literary Digest*, in an article detailing the results of a survey of Ukrainian Americans in 1919, reported that immigrants' "children receive their education in our public schools and . . . more often than not . . . these children of Ukrainian descent grow up with only a fractional knowledge of the Ukrainian tongue."

The Language of Compromise

As more and more Ukrainian Americans claimed English as their native tongue, other institutions slowly took measures to accommodate the younger generation. In the 1920s, the Ukrainian press began to shift the emphasis of its stories to address American as well as

The first and second graders of St. George's Ukrainian Catholic School in New York City in 1945. Ukrainian parish schools helped preserve the traditions and culture of the homeland by teaching the Ukrainian language and providing religious instruction.

European issues. In 1925, the Ukrainian National Association (UNA) published the first English-language Ukrainian magazine, *Juvenile*, aimed, as its title indicates, at young readers. The publication folded in the 1930s, bankrupted by the Great Depression. Soon after—in 1933—the UNA supplemented its daily newspaper, *Svoboda*, with the English-language *Ukrainian Weekly*. The new publication was initially condemned by critics, who viewed it as a sign that the UNA had "abandoned the Ukrainian language," but later it came to be seen as an important addition to the Ukrainian press.

Although many Ukrainians struggled to keep their language alive in North America, pressure has often been exerted on them to give it up, particularly during World War I, when widespread sentiment against foreigners resulted in campaigns to abolish all alien languages. In 1916, zealots threw bilingual books onto a bonfire on the grounds of the Manitoba legislature. Two years later, the Canadian government's censorship board, after monitoring Ukrainian publications for three years, suppressed them entirely. In 1919, bilingual schools were banned in Manitoba, Saskatchewan, and Alberta, the three provinces with the greatest concentration of Ukrainians in Canada. Such actions discouraged, but failed to eliminate, the use of the Ukrainian language.

New Generations

"I was born American, raised Ukrainian and my status is Canadian—a hyphenated consciousness reinforced by anger and guilt," Natalka Husar, a Ukrainian-American artist, told an audience of artists and critics in 1981. Many second-generation Ukrainians echo these feelings. Unlike their parents, who had vivid memories of Ukrainian life, those born in America have had to approach their own ethnicity as if it were a subject for study. Though called Ukrainian Americans, from birth they are more American than Ukrainian, simply as a result of the environment in which they live.

Ukrainian-language publications on display at a festival in New York City. Having learned English in order to prosper in the United States, Ukrainian Americans wish to ensure that the Ukrainian language survives in the New World.

Once they came of age, many Ukrainian Americans left the ethnic communities formed by their parents. Some even adopted anglicized names, perhaps because doing so caused other Americans to treat them less suspiciously, or perhaps because they themselves associated the ancestral name with poverty or ignorance. Those who changed their names—the only outward mark of their ethnic origin—often deprived themselves and their children of their cultural heritage.

Toward Full Americanization

Ukrainian-American organizations evolved through the generations. Ukrainian benevolent associations, the first to Americanize, did so more as a result of expansion than assimilation. As the Ukrainian immigrant population quickly increased and membership in the UNA grew, for example, so did the need for a more sophisticated life insurance system. Like other Ukrainian organizations that followed it, the UNA began to utilize modern actuarial insurance practices and offer different types of insurance policies.

As new generations of Ukrainian Americans were born, organizations formed to help integrate them into American society. Youth clubs played an important role. Most of these were originally founded as social organizations, and they provided a place where the offspring of immigrants—caught between the old culture and the new—could feel completely at home.

As Ukrainian Americans blended into mainstream America, their culture took on a new shape. The change did not please everyone. Some traditionalists, for example, objected to moving traditional dances from village squares to the stage, feeling that choreographer Avramenko sacrificed the original joy and meaning of the folk tradition in order to appeal to American audiences. "The minute you put something on stage and stylize it to make it presentable and enjoyable," complained Lusia Pavlychenko, director of the Saskatoon School of Ballet, "you take the folk out." By professionalizing the Ukrainian dance, Avramenko and his

Modern Ukrainian-American youth organizations help ease assimilation for the descendants of immigrants while promoting pride in their heritage.

followers transformed it from a locally interesting folk custom to fine art.

Urbanization also had an impact on Ukrainian folk music, which began to develop a sound that was more "American" and also up-to-date. Traditional harvest songs and seasonal songs, for example, reflect the experiences of pre-20th-century agrarian Ukrainians, but in the 1960s recordings of Ukrainian music began to reveal North American influences. The melodies remain traditional, but they are spiced with elements of jazz or rock and feature electric guitar and other modern instruments quite unlike the traditional *bandura*, the 30-stringed lutelike instrument that traditionally accompanied Ukrainian folk singing.

Old Meets New

Gradually—and sometimes unwillingly—Ukrainian Americans grew accustomed to American life. Yet they also clung to the culture and traditions of the land they had left behind. Faced with a conflict between old and

The annual street festival sponsored by New York City's Ukrainian community celebrates Ukrainian-American culture and tradition.

new, many Ukrainian Americans felt they must make an irrevocable choice between the two cultures. John Boswick (formerly Ivan Budzyck), a Canadian immigrant, came to America from the Ukraine before World War I. As one of his children later recalled, "I remember Mom saying that she had come to Canada to become a Canadian. So she wouldn't join their Ukrainian organization. . . . She said that they had all come over here to get away from the old ways and yet the first thing they wanted was to start them up over here again."

Most Ukrainian Americans, however, tried to navigate the difficult line between discarding the old and rejecting the new. They preserved those elements of their Ukrainian heritage most important to them, attempting to incorporate some of the old culture in the more immediate environment of their new homes.

Recently, Ukrainian Americans have worked to maintain many different ethnic traditions. As Wsevolod Isajiw, a sociology professor at the University of Toronto, indicated in a 1981 address to a conference on Ukrainians in Canada, one of the most prevalent of these maintained traditions among both second- and third-generation Ukrainian Americans is the preservation of the Ukrainian language. Results of a survey conducted by Isajiw indicated that more than 90 percent of second-generation Ukrainian Americans speak Ukrainian to their parents or children or have some general knowledge of the language, a much higher percentage than second-generation immigrants of other ethnic groups. In the third generation, the percentage falls to about 25 percent (and less than 10 percent read or write Ukrainian). Even this rate points to a greater emphasis and value placed on language than is evident in other immigrant groups. The 1970 U.S. census uncovered similar results: More than 60 percent of those who called Ukrainian their "mother tongue" were second- and third-generation Ukrainian Americans. The fact that they retain their language longer than other immigrant groups strongly indicates that Ukrainian

Americans see language as an important symbol of their cultural identity.

There are other strong links between past and present for Ukrainian Americans. According to Isajiw's survey, more than 81 percent of all third-generation Ukrainian Americans reported that they eat Ukrainian food on an everyday basis. More than a third practice traditional Ukrainian customs or participate in community functions, and nearly half of all third-generation Ukrainian Americans possess Ukrainian ornamental or artistic articles, such as pysanky, embroidered objects, and woodcarvings. Food, crafts, and works of art provide Ukrainian Americans with vivid and concrete reminders of their ethnic identity. With the help of these reminders, many have successfully bridged the gap between past and present.

Economic and Educational Improvement

Ukrainian Americans have made enormous economic and educational advances. In just over 100 years, they have developed from an impoverished, largely illiterate crowd of peasant farmers to an educated group of professionals, businesspeople, craftspeople and skilled workers, whose median income exceeded the national average by 12 percent in 1970.

Almost one-fourth of Ukrainian-American workers are professionals or administrators—a quantity actually lowered by the number of post-World War II immigrants (12.3 percent) engaged in such occupations. Ukrainian white-collar workers followed generations of ancestors in making a difficult but steady climb toward economic improvement. Those few first-generation immigrants who eventually completed their education in the United States had to work their way through school, but many were aided by scholarships provided by Ukrainian organizations and societies. By the 1930s, Ukrainians had dramatically improved their adult literacy rate, and most of these immigrants' children and grandchildren receive high school or college diplomas.

Traditional Ukrainian handicrafts, such as wood carvings and embroidery, can still be found in Ukrainian-American communities.

The inventive Ukrainian-American economist Simon Kuznets (right) accepts the Nobel Prize for economics from King Gustav Adolf of Sweden in December 1971.

Progress and Tradition

Ukrainian immigrants have contributed much to the continent that adopted them. In America, Ukrainian pioneers helped settle the north central states. In Canada, Ukrainian laborers tamed the western provinces and laid many miles of tracks for the Canadian Pacific Railway. In both countries, Ukrainians played a major role in the union movement. As they gained a foothold in North America, Ukrainians entered new fields—science, education, business, the arts, and the professions—where their influence spread, and individual Ukrainian Americans achieved prominence.

Simon Kuznets

Few people have had as great an impact on modern economic thought as Simon Kuznets, a Ukrainian American who won the Nobel Prize in Economics in 1971, the third year the prize was awarded. As originator of the concept of gross national product as a measure of a country's national income and economic growth, Kuznets has changed the methods of economic projection throughout the world.

The son of a fur dealer, Kuznets was born on April 30, 1901, in Kharkov, Ukraine, 250 miles southeast of Kiev. In 1907, Kuznets's father left six-year-old Simon and the rest of his family to seek his fortune in the United States. He planned to send for his family as soon as he could afford to, but the outbreak of World War I and the Russian Revolution altered his plans. Luckily, Simon Kuznets managed to attend secondary school, where he began his study of economics. At last, in 1922, 15 years after their separation, Simon and his father reunited in New York City.

The younger Kuznets enrolled in the graduate economics department of Columbia University and received his Ph.D. in 1926. He then joined the nonprofit National Bureau of Economic Research. In 1930, he was authorized by the U.S. Senate to collect estimates of national earnings and income levels in the United States. Kuznets thought this information might help clarify the damage done by the Great Depression, which had crippled the nation's economy. In compiling his data, Kuznets discovered that the national income had fallen almost 50 percent between 1929—when the stock market crashed—and 1932. He began to explore the possibility of using national income figures as the primary basis for economic studies of prosperity, depression, and growth potential. His work became the basis for the development of the concept of the gross national product (GNP), now used internationally as the standard index of a nation's wealth.

In later years, Kuznets studied the changing roles of capital, labor, and productivity. He also conducted a comprehensive study of income levels and patterns of the distribution of wealth in the United States during the postwar era. A teacher as well as a thinker, Kuznets sat on the faculties of major universities, including Harvard and Johns Hopkins. He retired from teaching in 1971. That same year he published *Economic Growth of Nations: Total Output and Production Structure*. It was widely acclaimed, and in December 1971 Kuznets was awarded the Nobel Prize in Economics. When he died in 1985, he was celebrated as a pioneer of modern economics whose work had proved that careful measurement and quantitative analysis could transform his chosen discipline into a more exact science.

George Kistiakowsky

Another important Ukrainian-American intellectual was George Kistiakowsky, a distinguished research chemist who later served as President Dwight D. Eisenhower's special assistant for science and technology. Kistiakowsky was born in Kiev on November 18, 1900, the son of a professor of international law at the University of Kiev. After attending schools in Kiev and Moscow, he fought against the Bolsheviks in the Russian Revolution. In the early 1920s Kistiakowsky made his way to Germany, where he attended the University of Berlin and obtained a Ph.D. in chemistry in 1925.

President Dwight D. Eisenhower (right) shares a laugh with his science adviser, Dr. George Kistiakowsky, in the summer of 1960. Born in Kiev, Kistiakowsky received a presidential citation for his contributions to the development of the atom bomb.

The following year, Kistiakowsky immigrated to the United States. He spent four years at Princeton University, first as a postdoctoral fellow in the department of physical chemistry and then as a research associate. In 1930, he joined the faculty of Harvard University, where he remained for more than 40 years. During a leave of absence in 1940, he worked as an explosives consultant for the National Defense Research Committee. Kistiakowsky did further work with explosives for the government during the early days of World War II. In 1943, he joined scores of other prominent scientists in Los Alamos, New Mexico, to work on the top secret Manhattan Project—the development of the world's first atomic bomb. Kistiakowsky's assignment was to prepare the conventional explosive used to detonate the bomb.

After receiving the president's Medal for Merit from Harry S. Truman in 1946, Kistiakowsky returned to Harvard, where he chaired the chemistry department for three years. He also resumed his research in physical chemistry, and during the next 25 years he wrote hundreds of articles for scientific journals. Kistiakowsky continued to serve the government in various advisory capacities as a member of the Department of Defense's Ballistic Missiles Advisory Committee and of the National Aeronautics and Space Administration's (NASA's) Chemical Energy Advisory Committee. In May 1959, President Dwight D. Eisenhower named him special assistant for science and technology. In that post, Kistiakowsky counseled the president on issues ranging from science education to coordination of the research and development performed by various government agencies. In 1961, when the Eisenhower administration ended, Kistiakowsky resumed his research and teaching at Harvard until his retirement.

Alexander Archipenko

Another Ukrainian American, Alexander Archipenko, combined a gift for science with a creative imagination to become one of the most innovative artists of the 20th

Avant-garde artist Alexander Archipenko and his wife, Angelica, waiting to set sail from Germany to the United States in 1923. A relentless innovator, Archipenko refused to be classified as a member of any particular artistic school.

century. He was born on May 30, 1887, the son of an engineering professor at the University of Kiev and the grandson of a painter who specialized in church murals. As a child, Archipenko admired the Byzantine frescoes and ancient icons of the Saint Sophia Cathedral in Kiev, and he went on to study painting and sculpture at the Kiev art school. In 1905, however, he was expelled for calling his professors "old-fashioned and academic." Undaunted, he continued his education elsewhere and soon became a trained engineer and an accomplished sculptor.

In 1908, Archipenko left his homeland for Paris, then the center of the art world, where he fell under the spell of Pablo Picasso and Georges Braque, whose cubist paintings—which renounced representational or realistic art in favor of an abstraction that sought to give an account of the whole structure of any given object and its position in space—were causing a sensation. Archipenko applied some of their innovations to sculpture and created purely geometric works. In 1910, he held a series of one-man exhibitions throughout Germany, where many museums purchased his sculptures. He then returned to Paris and in 1912 created "sculpto-painting," a new form that combined sculpture and painting. By 1923, when he immigrated to New York City, Archipenko had created hundreds of works of art and established art schools in Paris and Berlin.

In 1928, he became a naturalized U.S. citizen, and the following decade he taught at the University of Washington and the New Bauhaus School of Industrial Arts in Chicago. Archipenko's sculpture was prominently featured in the Ukrainian Pavilion at the 1933 World's Fair, which also highlighted Ukrainian music, dance, and food. During World War II, the works he had sold in Germany came under fire by the Nazis, who declared them "decadent." Almost every piece of his sculpture on display in museums was confiscated, along with 22 of his paintings. Most of these works were never recovered.

Archipenko remained in the United States and continued teaching, lecturing, and sculpting throughout

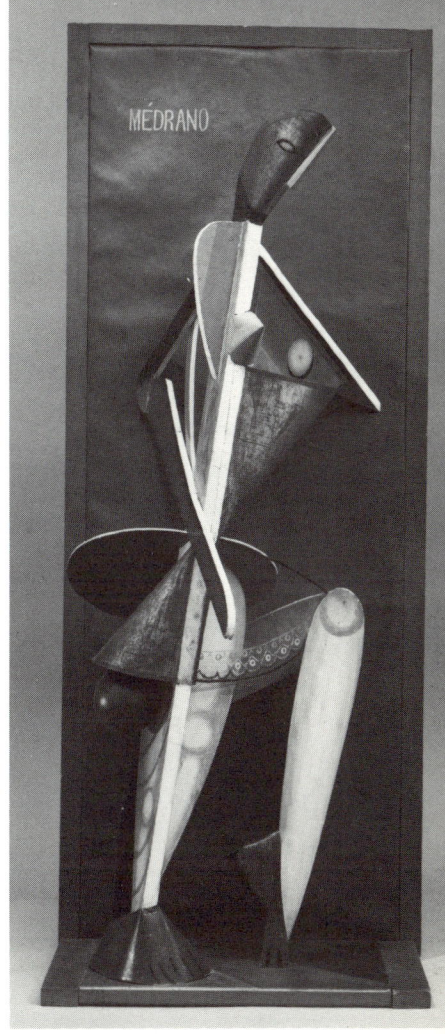

Archipenko's 1915 sculpture Medrano, *made of tin, glass, wood, and oilcloth, is part of the collection in New York City's Guggenheim Museum.*

the 1940s and 1950s. In 1948, he introduced "modeling light," a concept that makes space itself a form of sculpture. Archipenko compared the importance of space as an element in sculpture with the importance of a rest in music. His wealth of ideas led him to cross the boundaries of many established schools of art. As he once told an interviewer, "I never belonged to schools; I was expelled from schools. I did research, I invented and experimented." By the time he died in 1964, Archipenko had held 119 one-man exhibits throughout the world and had transformed the world's conception of sculpture.

Jack Palance

Just as Archipenko contributed to fine art, another Ukrainian American made an important contribution to popular art. Indeed, Jack Palance became the most famous entertainer of Ukrainian descent in the 20th century, starring on stage, screen, and television. Born Walter Palaniuk in 1920, the son of a Lattimer, Pennsylvania, coal miner, Palance won a football scholarship to the University of North Carolina, but he left before graduating to become a professional boxer. After serving in the U.S. Army Air Corps during World War II, Palance returned to America and decided to pursue a theatrical career.

Palance struggled for several years in New York City trying to land roles on the Broadway stage. He got his first break in 1950, when he made his screen debut in *Panic in the Streets*. Palance has starred in more than 40 movies, often playing a villain or tough guy. His performances in *Sudden Fear* (1952) and *Shane* (1953) netted him Oscar nominations for best supporting actor. His motion picture stardom enabled Palance to make a triumphant second try at the stage, where he appeared in William Shakespeare's *Julius Caesar* and *The Tempest* and in Tennessee Williams's *A Streetcar Named Desire*. Palance's greatest fame, however, has come through his work in television. His performance in Rod Serling's *Requiem for a Heavyweight* in the late

The rugged good looks of Ukrainian-American actor Jack Palance helped make him a star of stage, screen, and television for almost four decades.

1950s won him a Sylvania Award (predecessor of the Emmy), and in the 1960s, he was featured in many television movies as well as in the short-lived series "The Greatest Show on Earth" (1963). Palance starred in his own detective series, "Bronk," from 1975–76 before hosting the "Ripley's Believe It or Not" series in the 1980s. He is also an amateur poet and songwriter and in this capacity has staged recitals and made public appearances on behalf of various Ukrainian relief committees.

Mike Ditka

Another successful Ukrainian-American performer is football player and coach Mike Ditka, who was an all-American in college, a starring tight end for championship professional football teams, and the coach of the 1986 Super Bowl champion Chicago Bears. Ditka was born on October 18, 1939, in Carnegie, Pennsylvania, where his grandfather—a Ukrainian immigrant who had changed his name from Dyzcko—and his father both worked in a local steel mill.

Ditka escaped the poverty and hardship of the Pennsylvania steel mills by winning a college football

Elected to the National Football League Hall of Fame for his achievements as a player, Mike Ditka has earned equal success as a coach. Ditka has said that the fiery determination that has been his trademark was born watching how hard his father and grandfather had to work to earn a living.

scholarship to the University of Pittsburgh. He intended to continue his studies in the university's dentistry program, but his talent on the gridiron changed his plans. In 1961, following his junior year, he declared his availability in the professional draft and was claimed by the Chicago Bears of the National Football League (NFL). A superb tight end, he was named Rookie of the Year and went on to play a major role on the Bears 1963 championship team. The next year, Ditka set a record for tight ends by catching 75 passes despite a dislocated left shoulder that forced him to snare every ball with one hand. Injuries continued to plague him, but his career was far from over. He stayed with the Bears until 1966, played two seasons with the Philadelphia Eagles, and then was traded to the Dallas Cowboys in 1969. As a Cowboy, Ditka played in two Super Bowls—in 1971 and 1972—and scored a touchdown in the second, a Dallas victory over the Miami Dolphins.

The following year Ditka retired and took a job as an assistant coach for the Cowboys from 1973 to 1981. As offensive coordinator, Ditka helped head coach Tom Landry develop the famed "shotgun" formation that made Dallas "America's team" throughout the 1970s. In 1981, Ditka was named head coach of the Chicago Bears and led the team on a steady climb out of the cellar. When in 1986 the Bears won their first Super Bowl, Ditka was named NFL Coach of the Year by both the Associated Press (AP) and the *Sporting News* and was elected to the National Football Foundation's College Football Hall of Fame.

Kaye Lani Rae Rafko

A milestone in Ukrainian-American assimilation came on September 19, 1987, when Kaye Lani Rae Rafko was named Miss America 1988. The daughter of a Ukrainian-American father who owns a truck and auto parts business in Monroe, Michigan, and a mother of Irish and Welsh descent, Rafko was born on August

26, 1963. Rafko told the *Ukrainian Weekly* that her Ukrainian background "was always a part of me," fondly remembering the *pyrohy*—Ukrainian dumplings stuffed with a meat, cheese, or vegetable filling—made in her home twice a month as her "favorite dish."

Rafko first entered a local beauty pageant in 1981, hoping to raise money for her college tuition. The first prize of $700 financed her first year at a local college. Rafko entered other pageants throughout her college years, finishing first in a Michigan state pageant that brought her $1,500. Rafko had won over $10,000 in scholarship money from various local and state contests when she won the Miss America crown and its $30,000 prize.

In 1985, Rafko received her registered nurse diploma from St. Vincent Medical Center. Unlike previous Miss Americas, Rafko already had an established career when she won the title of Miss America. As a nurse, she has devoted particular attention to caring for terminally ill cancer and AIDS patients. Rafko hopes to use her prize money to further her studies in oncology (the study of tumors).

Ukrainian Americans have traveled a long journey from poverty, illiteracy, and despair to achievement in almost every field of American endeavor. In the beginning, many Ukrainian immigrants arrived in America hopeful of making their fortune but intent on returning to their homeland. Today, most Ukrainian Americans have resolved to remain in North America, though they have not forgotten the old country and still hope for an independent Ukraine.

Most members of the community have managed both to join the mainstream culture and to participate in a thriving ethnic community. The importance Ukrainian Americans place on their ethnic heritage and on passing their traditions on to younger generations augurs well for the survival of Ukrainian tradition and culture.

A tearful Kaye Lani Rae Rafko moments after learning that she had been named Miss America for 1988.

FURTHER READING

Bratush, James D. *A Historical Documentary of the Ukrainian Community of Rochester, New York.* Rochester, NY: Christopher Press, 1973.

Dolot, Miron. *Execution by Hunger: The Hidden Holocaust.* New York: Norton, 1985.

———. *Echoing Trails: Billings County History.* Medora, ND: Billings County Historical Society, 1979.

Halich, Wasyl. *Ukrainians in the United States.* San Francisco: A & E Research Associates, 1969.

Luciuk, Lubomyr Y. *Ukrainians in the Making: Their Kingston Story.* Kingston, Ontario: Limestone Press, 1980.

Lupul, Manoly R., ed. *Visible Symbols: Cultural Expression Among Canada's Ukrainians.* Edmonton, Alberta: Canadian Institute of Ukrainian Studies, 1984.

Martynowych, Orest T. *The Ukrainian Bloc Settlement in East Central Alberta, 1890–1930: A History.* Alberta, Canada: Alberta Culture, 1985.

Wertsman, Vladimir, ed. *The Ukrainians in America 1608–1975: A Chronology & Fact Book.* Dobbs Ferry, NY: Oceana Publications, 1976.

Index

Alaska, 47, 48
Alaska Herald and Svoboda, 48
Alexander II, 26–27
Alexis I, 25
Ameryka, 73, 78
Archipenko, Alexander, 102–3
Austria-Hungary, 28–29, 58
Avramenko, Vasyl, 81

Bandera, Stefan, 34
Bandura, 95
Bohachovsky, Konstantin, 74
Bohoon, Lawrenty, 47
Bolsheviks, 27, 28, 30
Boyars, 21
Brest-Litovsk, Treaty of, 28
Bukovina, 30, 34
Byzantine architecture, 20–21

California, 14, 48
Canada, Ukrainians in, 41–42, 45, 58–59, 62, 65, 66–67, 93
Carpatho-Ukraine, 30, 34
Catholicism. *See* Roman Catholics; Ukrainian Catholics
Charles XII, king of Sweden, 26
Chernobyl nuclear accident, 35
Civil War, American, 48
Communist party, 31
Connecticut, 14
Cossacks, 23–24, 25–26
Cyril and Methodius Society, 27
Cyrillic alphabet, 19, 79

Ditka, Mike, 105–6
Dnieper River, 20, 26
Dolot, Miron, 37, 85

Echoing Trails, 40, 43, 83
Elyniak, Wasyl, 41
Epoch of ruins, 25
Execution by Hunger: The Hidden Holocaust (Dolot), 37, 85

Five-Year Plan, 32
Florida, 14
Fort Ross, 48

Galicia, 29, 34, 38, 69, 74
Germany, 28, 33–34
Golden Horde, 22, 23
Gorbachev, Mikhail, 35
Goths, 19

Hawaiian Islands, 44
Herodotus, 19
Homestead Act, 39, 64
Honcharenko, Agapius, 48
Hromadas, 27
Huns, 19
Hurinenko, Julia Ann, 40, 43
Husar, Natalka, 93

Illinois, 14
Isajiw, Wsevolod, 96
Ivan III, prince of Muscovy, 23

Jamestown, 47
Juvenile, 93

Khan, Batu, 22
Kharkov, 28
Khmelnytsky, Bohdan, 25
Khrushchev, Nikita, 35
Kiev, 19
Kievan Russia, 20–23
Kistiakowsky, George, 101–2
Kodiak Island, 26
Konowal, Philip, 66
Koshetz, Alexander, 81
Kuznets, Simon, 99–100

Lenin, Vladimir Ilyich, 27
Lithuania, 24
Luciuk, Lubomyr K., 58

Marx, Karl, 30
Mazepa, Ivan, 26
Michigan, 14, 65
Mongols, 22
Muscovy, 23–25

New Jersey, 14, 58
New York, 14, 58
Nicholas I, czar of Russia, 26

Nicholas II, czar of Russia, 27
North Dakota, 40, 64–66
Novgorod, 20

Ohio, 14
Oleg, 20
Ortynsky, Stephen Soter, 73–74

Palance, Jack, 104–5
Palaniuk, Beverly, 66
Pavlychenko, Lusia, 94
Pennsylvania, 14, 47, 58, 61
Perestroika, 35
Peter I, czar of Russia, 26
Petlyura, Simon, 29
Petrograd, 27
Plast, 89
Poland, 24, 25, 26, 29
Pylypiw, Ivan, 41–42
Pysanky, 82

Rada, 27–29
Rafko, Kaye Lani Rae, 106–7
Republic of Western Ukraine, 29
Revolutionary war, American, 48
Roman Catholics, 21, 24
Romanians, 30–31
Rurik, 20
Rus, 20
Russian Orthodox Church, 26–27
Russification, 31
Russkaya Pravda, 22
Ruthenia, 74
"Ruthenian," 69

St. Nicholas Brotherhood, 76
Scythia, 19
Sembratovich, Cardinal, 72
Shevchenko Day, 82
Shevchenko, Taras, 27
Sifton, Clifford, 45
Skoropadsky, Paul, 28
Slavic people, 19
Smith, John, 47
Soviet Union, 29–35
Stalin, Joseph, 31–35
Stundinsts, 27, 60
Surma Book and Music Company, 81

Sutter, John, 48
Svoboda, 78, 93

Takach, Wasyl, 74
Tatars, 23
Toth, Alex, 73
Trylovsky, Kyrylo, 78

Ukraine
  collective farms, 33
  emigration of people, 39–45
  famine of the 1920s, 32
  farming, 38–39
  history of, 19–35
  independence of, 13, 17
  natural resources of, 17–18
  opposition to emigration from, 34, 43
  oppressors of, 17
  population of, 17
  size of, 17
  Soviet control, 30–35
  tribes of, 18–19
  village life, 37
Ukrainian Aid Association, 78
Ukrainian Americans
  areas of residence in U.S., 14, 58
  boardinghouses of, 62
  in Canada, 41–42, 45, 58–59, 62, 65, 66–67, 93
  churches, functions of, 71
  community organizations, 75–78, 88–89, 94
  crafts, 82, 97
  early immigrants, 47–57
  educational achievement, 97
  English language learning, 91–92
  and farming, 64–66
  folk culture, 80–82, 94–95
  holidays, 82–83
  hostility toward, 44–45, 58, 66, 93
  income of, 15, 97
  internment during World War I, 58, 66–67
  journey to America, 43–45
  and labor movement, 14, 59–60, 61, 63
  in mining industry, 61–63

110   THE UKRAINIAN AMERICANS

nationality issue, 13–14, 69
old/new ways, conflict between, 94–97
parish schools, 92
as pioneers, 14
political activism, 88–89
press/newspapers, 78–80, 92–93
prominent Ukrainian Americans, 99–107
railway companies and, 62–63
religion, 71–75
second-generation, feelings of, 93–94
success of, 15–16
Ukrainian language, preservation of, 96–97
waves of immigration, 39–41, 57–59, 86–88
World War II period, 85–88
Ukrainian Baptists, 75
Ukrainian Catholics, 13, 21–22, 24, 71–74
Ukrainian Jews, 34
Ukrainian Museum, 76–77
Ukrainian National Association (UNA), 76, 93, 94
Ukrainian National Chorus, 81
Ukrainian Nationalists, Organization of, 34
Ukrainian National Republic, 27–30, 42, 70
Ukrainian National Women's League of America (UNWLA), 76
Ukrainian National Youth Federation (UNYF), 78
Ukrainian Orthodox, 13, 75
Ukrainian People's church, 75
Ukrainian Protestants, 75
Ukrainians in the Making (Luciuk), 58
Ukrainian Weekly, 93
Ukrainian Youth League of North America, 77–78

Vikings, 20
Vladimir I, prince of Kiev, 20
Volansky, John, 72–73, 76
Volynia, 29
Vyhovsky, Ivan, 25

Wisconsin, 65
World War I, 28–30, 42, 58, 66–67
World War II, 33–34

Xatas, 38

Yaroslav the Wise, prince of Kiev, 21

Zaporizhska Sich, 24

Picture Credits

We would like to thank the following sources for providing photographs: Alinari/Art Resource: p. 26; The Bettmann Archive: pp. 41, 104; Frances Archipenko Gray: p. 102; Solomon Guggenheim Museum: p. 103; Immigration History Research Center, University of Minnesota, St. Paul: pp. 43, 80; Library of Congress: pp. 27, 38, 48, 60, 61; Manitoba Archives: pp. 46–47, 58, 63, 65, 71; Minnesota Historical Society: pp. 84–85; Multicultural History Society of Ontario Photograph Collection, Archives of Ontario: p. 15; National Archives: p. 87; National Archives of Canada: pp. 44, 45; National Park Service, Statue of Liberty National Monument: p. 70; Orthodox Church in America Archives: p. 74; Österreichische National-bibliothek, Vienna: p. 22; Provincial Archives of Alberta: cover, pp. 12–13; St. Lawrence Parks Commission/Old Fort Henry, Kingston, Ontario: p. 67; Donna Sinisgalli: p. 18; Slavonic Division, New York Public Library, Astor, Lenox and Tilden Foundation: p. 25; Sovfoto: pp. 16–17, 19, 21, 25, 30, 33, 34; Katrina Thomas: pp. 49, 50, 51, 52, 53, 54, 55, 56, 82, 90–91, 93, 95, 96, 97; Ukrainian Cultural and Educational Association, Winnipeg: pp. 36–37, 43, 62; Ukrainian Museum of New York: pp. 29, 31, 32, 39, 40, 57, 68–69, 72, 73, 75, 77, 79, 86, 88, 92; UPI/Bettmann Newsphotos: pp. 98–99, 101, 105, 107

KEVIN OSBORN is a free-lance writer and editor who has coauthored several volumes in the American Heritage *History of the United States* series. The author of many other books for children and adults, he also helped create the characters for the young adult fiction series *Not Quite Human*, which was the basis for a Disney Productions television movie of the same name.

DANIEL PATRICK MOYNIHAN is the senior United States senator from New York. He is also the only person in American history to serve in the cabinets or subcabinets of four successive presidents—Kennedy, Johnson, Nixon, and Ford. Formerly a professor of government at Harvard University, he has written and edited many books, including *Beyond the Melting Pot*, *Ethnicity: Theory and Experience* (both with Nathan Glazer), *Loyalties*, and *Family and Nation*.